Cambridge Elements ≡

Elements in Public and Nonprofit Administration
edited by
Andrew Whitford
University of Georgia
Robert Christensen
Brigham Young University

T0312046

LEADERSHIP
STANDPOINTS

A Practical Framework for the Next Generation of Nonprofit Leaders

Don Waisanen
Baruch College, City University of New York

CAMBRIDGE
UNIVERSITY PRESS

CAMBRIDGE
UNIVERSITY PRESS

University Printing House, Cambridge CB2 8BS, United Kingdom

One Liberty Plaza, 20th Floor, New York, NY 10006, USA

477 Williamstown Road, Port Melbourne, VIC 3207, Australia

314–321, 3rd Floor, Plot 3, Splendor Forum, Jasola District Centre,
New Delhi – 110025, India

103 Penang Road, #05–06/07, Visioncrest Commercial, Singapore 238467

Cambridge University Press is part of the University of Cambridge.

It furthers the University's mission by disseminating knowledge in the pursuit of
education, learning, and research at the highest international levels of excellence.

www.cambridge.org
Information on this title: www.cambridge.org/9781009001113
DOI: 10.1017/9781009000284

First published 2021

A catalogue record for this publication is available from the British Library.

ISBN 978-1-009-00111-3 Paperback
ISSN 2515-4303 (online)
ISSN 2515-429X (print)

Leadership Standpoints

A Practical Framework for the Next Generation of Nonprofit Leaders

Elements in Public and Nonprofit Administration

DOI: 10.1017/9781009000284
First published online: September 2021

Don Waisanen
Baruch College, City University of New York
Author for correspondence: Don Waisanen, don.waisanen@baruch.cuny.edu

Abstract: This project offers a new leadership framework for the next generation of nonprofit professionals. Based on five years of data collected from the New York Community Trust Leadership Fellowship – designed to address leadership development gaps in the nonprofit sector – it constructs three dimensions and eleven themes for the theory and practice of *leadership standpoints*. Leadership standpoints are a framework for practicing inclusion, building spaces for performance, and thinking and acting with range. Those using leadership standpoints continuously interact with diverse stakeholders, constantly verify others' views and interests, and remain keenly attentive to power distributions, material constraints, and hidden or unacknowledged voices that need surfaced, while expanding their personal and social outlooks to elevate performance and meet pressing demands best addressed through broadly informed decisions. This title is also available as Open Access on Cambridge Core.

This Element also has a video abstract: www.cambridge.org/waisanen

Keywords: leadership, inclusion, diversity, nonprofit, standpoint

ISBNs: 9781009001113 (PB), 9781009000284 (OC)
ISSNs: 2515-4303 (online), 2515-429X (print)

Contents

1 Introduction: The Crucible of Nonprofit Leadership

It is important for people to have time to reflect on the type of leader that they are, the type of leader they want to be, how their leadership styles impact how a program or an organization works and runs, and where there are gaps in their leadership . . . being transparent with yourself and others . . . and then finding people, talented people, who can bridge that gap.

New York Community Trust Leadership Fellows Alumnus

In the last few years, Deborah has worked at a number of nonprofits in New York. She has delivered critical services for people in the community; held administrative assistant positions for an after-school program dedicated to closing gaps in educational inequalities; worked at a healthcare organization providing medical supplies for the uninsured; supported attorneys offering free legal advice to immigrants; and, in her latest job, helped low-income families gain access to healthy food. Given these experiences and being great at what she does, six months into her new job the executive director offers Deborah a promotion to a position of leadership within the organization. While she's certainly excited by many of the job's perks, such as an increased salary, Deborah has long looked forward to moving into a position with greater responsibility, so accepts the offer quickly. However, after the first year of trying to manage people and develop new initiatives, she runs into a series of headache-inducing challenges.

These include a high turnover rate of direct reports; low staff performance; a continued lack of board buy-in for needed organizational changes; fudged financial reports and lower than expected fundraising projections; increasing concerns about racial and gender disparities between administrators and the people that the nonprofit serves; and, as a result, an increasingly cynical climate, escalating conflicts, and morale that's spiraling downward. Deborah finds herself in the midst of a "crucible" experience, where one's abilities are so tested and adversity runs so high that extraordinary insight and growth are demanded (Bennis & Thomas 2002). Having had little training in leadership to begin with, she wonders what she could have done differently, and, more important, what she could do in the future to become the type of leader she'd aspired to be.

As played out every day across the nonprofit sector, this situation begs a simple question with high stakes: What type of leadership should the next generation of nonprofit professionals hope to develop? Few other issues will affect the day-to-day life of organizations and societies as much as their leaders. When people are given the knowledge to lead well they feel empowered, gain clarity and focus, inspire others, build inclusive and trustful communities, and accomplish all that their mission, vision, and values set forth. On the other hand, when people lack leadership skills, the results can be disastrous. If there's any area of professional development you wouldn't want to leave to chance, this would be it.

1.1 The Nonprofit Leadership Deficit

This Element provides the next generation of nonprofit professionals with a state-of-the-art, practical approach to leadership. It will be of interest to emerging nonprofit leaders looking for a broad and deep blueprint from which to operate, as well as long-standing nonprofit leaders looking to revise or bring their leadership ideas and actions more fully into the twenty-first century. It will also be of interest to scholars and other practitioners interested in nonprofit leadership, and especially those working in nonprofit leadership development that has often lacked through lines, remained static in the face of diverse and changing contexts, or failed to speak holistically to the needs of nonprofit professionals. *Leadership standpoints* provide a guiding, open-ended framework for both leadership development programs and leadership in action.

A host of research concludes that rising professionals need leadership development (Aguinis & Kraiger 2009; Chenok et al. 2017; Collins & Holton 2004; Conger 2010; Getha-Taylor et al. 2015; Lacerenza et al. 2017; Pernick 2001; Seidle, Fernandez, & Perry 2016) or the expansion of an individual's and collective's "capacity to be effective in leadership roles and processes" (McCauley, Van Velsor, & Ruderman 2010: 2, 20). In the nonprofit sector, however, leadership development has long been difficult to address, given its tight budgets and limited resources. Some studies show that nearly 70 percent of executives may leave the nonprofit sector in the near future.[1] Describing this nonprofit leadership development deficit, research finds that "Succession planning is the No. 1 organizational concern of US nonprofits, but they are failing to develop their most promising pool of talent: homegrown leaders," while "demand for effective nonprofit leaders today is as high as ever" (Landles-Cobb, Kramer, & Milway 2015: paras. 1, 5; Norley & D'Amato 2019). Furthermore, it's not simply a matter of filling previous roles but of increasing the leadership capacities of more people at all levels. As many organizational structures become flatter and more team-based, the demands for distributing leadership among staff have increased. Smaller nonprofits, where employees perform many roles, only heighten this need (Hernez-Broome & Hughes 2004; Leskiw & Singh 2007).

---

[1] See the Robert Morris University Bayer Center for Nonprofit Management report *What Now: How Will the Impending Retirement of Nonprofit Leaders Change the Sector* (2018), https://bcnm .rmu.edu/ProgramsServices/cmp-media/docs/BayerCenter/bayercenterwhatnowretirementfin dingsjan27_2018final.pdf.

Although gaps in nonprofit leadership development continue to remain a national concern, New York State alone provides a jarring example of how these fissures have widened as the sector continues to grow. A report on nonprofit organizations found "New York led the nation in both the number of people employed by nonprofits and total wages paid by these organizations" (at about 18 percent of private employment in 2017), and "From 2007 through 2017, these entities added more than 175,000 jobs in New York, a gain of 14 percent. During and after the Great Recession, they helped stabilize overall employment as jobs declined elsewhere in the private sector and among governmental employers" (DiNapoli 2019: 1). It's thus more important than ever to develop leadership across the nonprofit sector.

Focusing on staff retention and advancement will remain critical to these efforts. Many people leave nonprofit positions due to the lack of opportunities for learning, mentoring, and growth. The need to "recognize the enormity of the problem and make it a top priority" stems from several factors involving limited supply and burgeoning demand: "the growing number of nonprofit organizations, the retirement of managers from the vast baby-boomer generation, the movement of existing nonprofit managers into different roles within or outside the sector, and the growth in the size of nonprofits" (Tierney 2006: paras. 9, 7; Le 2019: paras. 7–8). Overall, as Peggy Outen notes: "We see a sector that seldom calls the hiring process talent acquisition, a sector that too infrequently grows its own into leadership – a sector that is relentlessly outwardly focused, [and] now challenged to up its game internally to meet a demanding future" (Lindstrom 2018: para. 5). On a more positive note, these trends have attracted the attention of funders seeking to address nonprofit leadership development. Their efforts are paving the way for how to address deficits, while also raising questions about the type of leadership best suited to nonprofit professionals.

1.2 The Importance of a Nonprofit Leadership Theory

With the largest number of nonprofits of any city in the United States, New York City has provided a test case for foundations and other donors to fill the leadership development gap and build support for nonprofit professionals. The New York Community Trust Leadership Fellows (NYCTLF) program is one such effort. Begun in 2015 and funded entirely by the New York Community Trust (in collaboration with the Baruch College, City University of New York Marxe School of Public and International Affairs),[2] the program has trained fall and spring cohorts of nonprofit professionals in leadership

---

[2] There is a large literature on the need for universities to be involved in such work (e.g. Diner 2017; Maurrasse 2001; van der Wusten 1998).

development since its inception. The twelve-week certificate program includes seminars with practitioners and professors, a hands-on curriculum addressing the needs of nonprofit professionals in areas from communication to finance, a core change project that each fellow undertakes on behalf of their organization over the fellowship's course, individual pairings with mentors who have decades of field experience, and dinner conversations and networking events with leaders in the nonprofit and government sectors.[3] Figure 1 shows one of the fellowship's cohorts (Sperrazza 2019).

A participant once shared with me that the fellowship was the "Rosetta Stone" for her career and promotion into leadership positions. Yet, beyond the anecdotes, more systematic analysis has also been undertaken. In the first four years of the NYCTLF, an evaluation was conducted to identify the program's strengths and areas for improvement. The report examined all aspects of the fellowship in terms of its stated goals, namely to "increase the quality and diversity of leadership talent available to nonprofit organizations, with a priority focus on leaders of color" and to "improve the knowledge, skills, and confidence of mid-career professionals so that they become more effective managers and change leaders

Figure 1 A New York Community Trust Leadership Fellows (NYCTLF) cohort

---

[3] See paragraph 4 of the "About Us" section of the New York Community Trust Leadership Fellowship website: https://trustfellows.org/about-us/. In terms of recruitment, nominations of emerging leaders are made by the executive director or another senior staff member of current trust grantees. Fellows are then selected and invited to join the upcoming cohort. Potential nominating organizations cut across the different, broad nonprofit areas of the trust's interests.

Figure 2 NYCTLF leadership training. Photo courtesy of the NYCTLF.

within their organizations" (Reinelt & Fried 2018a: 3).[4] Over approximately two years, the evaluators carried out surveys, focus groups, and more with past and current cohorts, program faculty, and other stakeholders to capture the program's perceived impacts and make recommendations for future planning.

In addition to continuing assessments of the participants' experiences across the program by NYCTLF staff, the fellows, instructors, and program stakeholders identified a significant need for the fellowship, with broad applicability to the nonprofit sector: to develop a theory or framework for leadership for the program as a whole and as a contribution to the field of leadership and nonprofit professional development writ large. A report implied that there may be an underlying theory about leadership already implicit in the program, or at least a model or framework that could be created and articulated more intentionally (Reinelt & Fried 2018b: 1, 2). Having such a theory would follow the grounding in existing literature for value- and diversity-based leadership as a starting point for nonprofits, provide a through line for the many different topics that make up leadership development (e.g. organizational development, communication, finance, management, etc.) and provide a memorable imprint to guide participants' practice (see Figure 2).

From another perspective, the literature on training and development makes clear that having a model to guide program objectives is critical to carrying out this type of work effectively. All professional development programs should be

[4] The trust's impact assessment report can be found here: www.nycommunitytrust.org/newsroom/a-report-on-the-new-york-community-trust-leadership-fellows/.

"working from a solid theoretical framework and thoughtfully allowing empirical knowledge to guide ... decisions," which makes them "credible, effective, and valuable to the organizations which seek their help" (Waldeck & Seibold 2016: xi). Conger (2010: 289–290) advises that leadership development programs should be built "*around a single well-delineated leadership model*" (emphasis added)[5] based on studies demonstrating participants' learning is improved through a clear focus on behaviors and competencies and different content, learning methods, and assessments taking place over multiple sessions, with organizational and other reinforcements in place.

In essence, there is "no theory-free consulting; we are all driven by explicit and/or implicit human and organizational theories" (Pettegrew 2016: 308), and using guiding theories impacts leadership, management, and self-assessments (Sasnett & Ross 2007). Those in the professional development space hence need to be more strategic about the theories that guide their work (Gale 2018; Jackson & Aakhus 2014; Waisanen 2019). Under these terms, nonprofit professionals need a leadership theory that's descriptive and normative – providing both a guide for mapping their experiences and a lens to assess their daily practices.[6] With these purposes in mind, let's turn to the modeling function that such a theory can serve.

1.3 Modeling Nonprofit Leadership

Having observed firsthand the impact that leadership programs leave on their participants and alumni, I've long thought about the topic, particularly from the perspective of communication practice. As a teacher of both leadership and communication in a variety of programs and schools, and having been with the NYCTLF as a faculty member and mentor since its start, the question of what type of nonprofit leadership should be modeled became more pronounced in my own experiences over time. In discussions with many practitioners and scholars in this space, too, it became clear that we need to know more and can do better when it comes to articulating a vision for nonprofit leadership.

With more than five years of program data, the NYCTLF has been well positioned to express a distinct theory of leadership for nonprofit professional development. There are many theories of leadership (e.g. transformational, situational, adaptive, servant leadership, etc.; Northouse 2018) that are certainly useful and can be incorporated into such a model. Yet, given the results of

---

[5] Emphasis added.

[6] For any big term like "leadership" that tries to capture more than we are ever able to fully capture in words, we are trying to get at what scholars call a pragmatic theory of the middle range (Watts 2011) – a snapshot of contextualized practices that contribute to the overall picture. This project was engineered with this approach in mind.

assessments in the last several years, what became clear is that a leadership theory that speaks to the depth and breadth of participants' aspirations, the many different teachings and practices that have emerged from subject matter experts within the program, the evolving online knowledge hub constructed by both program staff and the fellows themselves, and especially the finding that the program needs social justice–oriented themes to carry across the program, all beg the question of what theory of leadership could best encapsulate this wealth of experience and education. This theory looks both inward to the many learnings that have taken place across the program and outward to the literatures on leadership, related fields, and other professional development programs from which further insights can be derived.

Before going further, it's worth mentioning that you cannot *not* have a theory or theories of leadership operating in an organization – you can see it in everything that people say and do.[7] If, for example, Derek, the executive director of a local nonprofit, never seeks input from staff when it comes time to devising a strategic plan, never allows board members to speak at the annual gala, and frequently can be heard making comments such as "we don't need to hear more voices, we need results," he's clearly channeling an authoritarian theory of leadership. So one goal of this work is to get more strategic and less ad hoc or intuitional about the theories of leadership already at work in nonprofit planning and action.

In this sense, another goal of this project is to simply make nonprofit leadership less nebulous. To construct a definition for leadership, this study seeks to not merely identify and fill a gap but to build on the values that have become foundational to the NYCTLF fellowship, similar programs, and current trends in leadership research emphasizing the need for distributed and connective models that put the exercise of leadership within all people's reach (Gronn 2002; Pearce & Conger 2002).

Since the organizational change literature is clear that "what works well in one organization, culture, or country, may well produce failure in another organization, culture, or country" (Jacobs, Van Witteloostuijn, & Christe-Zeyse 2013: 775), a theory that remains sensitive to contexts and diverse people and cultures is integral to this visioning. At the same time, it's worth recognizing from the outset that definitions can be tyrannical. I certainly don't want to force a closed and conclusive definition of leadership in this project that fails to account for future learnings. In constructing a theory, there's a paradox in both needing to draw from and develop useful ideas for leadership while being

---

[7] I draw inspiration here from Pearce (2009) and the adage that "you cannot not communicate" (Watzlawick, Beavin, & Jackson 1967: 49).

attentive to what the theory possibly excludes. In this spirit, and following the guidance offered by many of the dimensions and themes to come, I offer a flexible and open-ended definition for nonprofit leadership that welcomes future insights and amendments, contractions, or expansions.

Ultimately, this project puts forth a theory of *leadership standpoints* for the next generation of nonprofit professionals. Based on five years of data from a complete review of NYCTFL materials, including all surveys, focus groups, and similar data from its program evaluation, and drawing from leadership literatures and comparisons with similar leadership training programs, this Element creates a framework for leadership standpoints. As part of this effort, we conducted interviews with a random sample of NYCTFL alumni (and searched for patterns in these data through follow-up computer-aided textual analyses) and sought extensive feedback from program stakeholders, academics, and nonprofit practitioners every step of the way. These interviews stood at the tip of an iceberg, carrying all the previous work forward by helping to sharpen, distill, and extend many themes that were already percolating based on the prior evaluation work,[8] the broad review of program and external materials, and many conversations and seminars we engaged in to discuss this project's findings. Before getting into many of these details, let's first define leadership standpoints.

2 What Are Leadership Standpoints?

Before moving on to the connections between leadership standpoints and related leadership studies, as well as the specific features of the theory for nonprofit leadership development and practice, I'd like to provide a cursory definition and overview of the concept's dimensions and themes. In essence, a theory of leadership standpoints both describes and prescribes a form of nonprofit leadership keenly attentive to one's and others' positionalities at every turn. By positionality, I mean the many different standpoints from which one and others operate. Sánchez (2010: 2258) describes positionality as:

> [the] notion that personal values, views, and location in time and space influence how one understands the world. In this context, gender, race, class, and other aspects of identities are indicators of social and spatial positions and are not fixed, given qualities. Positions act on the knowledge a person has about things, both material and abstract. Consequently, knowledge is the product of a specific position that reflects particular places and spaces.

---

[8] An executive summary of the NYCTLF program evaluation can be found at: www.nycommunity trust.org/newsroom/a-report-on-the-new-york-community-trust-leadership-fellows/.

This involves being aware of the positions from which each person thinks and acts, while also attending to the cognitive, affective, behavioral, structural, and environmental forces at play within and between people, organizations, and communities. For example, Fulton, Oyakawa, and Wood (2019: 260) find that "leaders of color can help predominantly white organizations work for racial equality by providing a 'critical standpoint' – an outsider-within perspective that allows them to see and critique racialized dimensions of organizational life" that can be difficult for others to see.

Leadership standpoints forward an aspirational purpose by advising that nonprofit leaders continually try to step into new standpoints to best enact their institution's mission, vision, and values. Grounded in current calls to forward "collective leadership development" that moves beyond individual performance and engages and extends "multiple entities in the leadership process" (Eva et al. 2019: 1), leadership standpoints are not simply about stepping into others' shoes but about identifying and continually trying to understand the variety of standpoints one and others inhabit to push beyond those boundaries and perform new standpoints. In this sense, leadership standpoints incorporate but are also larger than just "perspectives" or "views," terms that tend to have heady, cognitive connotations. Standpoints get at where we and others stand, with a focus on the material and ecological, not merely intellectual bases from which people engage with their worlds.

Since standpoints aren't fixed, what leadership standpoints add to the field is a moral, prescriptive lens that speaks to the foundational and emergent positions of nonprofit life, from long-standing, best practices in management to newer, participatory forms of organizational budgeting. It's grounded in practical ethics, since "inclusion and affective commitment" are "key factors for how leaders can increase nonprofit performance" (Brimhall 2019: 31). Leadership standpoints are about casting as wide a lens as possible on the contexts that we each inhabit, while constantly being ready to shift or deepen one's positions. Consistent with contemporary scholarship, leadership standpoints are not absolute nor intended to offer a one-size-fits-all approach but rather reflect a type of leadership that requires constant input and customizations to fully reflect today's organizational needs.[9]

---

[9] This follows literature arguing that "Leadership development is context-sensitive. There is no one best way to lead or to develop leaders. In different settings, there may be different expectations of leaders and different practices that make them effective." It is also "an ongoing process ... grounded in personal [and collective] development, which is never complete" (McCauley, Van Velsor, & Ruderman 2010: 3, 26). Leadership standpoints are dynamic rather than static and workable rather than perfectionistic. They also work with one of the largest studies of leadership ever conducted, which found that there are *both* clusters of expectations for leadership across the world and significant variations in different cultures. For example, almost universally people

In essence, *those applying leadership standpoints practice inclusion, build spaces for performance, and think and act with range.* To do so, such leaders continuously interact with diverse stakeholders, constantly verify others' views and interests, and remain keenly attentive to power distributions, material constraints, and hidden or unacknowledged voices that need surfaced, while expanding their personal and social outlooks to elevate performance and meet pressing demands best addressed through broadly informed decisions.

At its heart, each of these moves requires the expansion of one's own and others' positionalities. Inclusion requires the ongoing recognition and incorporation of others' positions into all aspects of leadership. Building spaces for performance constantly places all staff between the positions of what is and what could be. Thinking and acting with range asks the next generation of nonprofit leaders to continuously learn different positions through multiple methods and means. In Section 2.2, I detail two brief examples for what this line of leadership looks like in action and why it's well-suited to nonprofit leadership, in particular. Before doing so, to gain a deeper understanding of its dimensions and themes, let's take a look at the pluralistic background from which leadership standpoints stem.

2.1 Pluralistic Dimensions

From the data collected in this project, I use an intentional plurality in constructing leadership standpoints to underscore the emphasis on multiplicity observed throughout this project – the need for multiple voices, multiform interpretations, and multicultural understandings and applications in all leadership work. At the same time, I have drawn the term "standpoints" loosely from two theoretical lenses with their own histories and that align with the research findings.

The first, "standpoint theory," builds from three premises: that "knowledge is socially situated," that "marginalized groups are socially situated in ways that make it more possible for them to be aware of things and ask questions than it is for the non-marginalized," and that "research . . . should begin with the lives of the marginalized" (Bowell n.d.: para. 1).[10] Standpoint theory turns foremost to the voices of those typically excluded from decision-making to build inclusivity and gain a more accurate diagnosis of what's actually happening in any situation than would be available had this broad net not been cast. For this project's purposes, the theory would have practitioners maintain a laser-like focus on the

---

expect leaders to broadcast charisma, integrity, and interpersonal communication skills, while avoiding being nonsocial, malevolent, and self-focused. Yet these expectations play out in different ways across settings (Northouse 2015, adapted from Dorfman, Hanges, & Brodbeck 2004).

[10] Harding (2004) coined the term "standpoint theory."

positions (in behaviors, language, knowledge, structural positions, and other applications) from which they and others function, in the service of creating equitable, informed, and productive conditions for all that can best move a cause forward.

The second, what's been called "the viewpoints," is a theory grounded in training for performers, particularly dancers and actors. The theory trains performers to observe the elements of "space, shape, time, emotion, movement, and story" that make up the scenes of our lives.[11] Key to this is how "an ensemble using Viewpoints is likely to be more collaborative than a traditional cast in which performers and designers defer to the director's vision" (Hunter n.d.: para. 13). Relative to this project, the viewpoints stress collaboration and attention to one's ecology, symbols, and embodied human performance. They also highlight the structural impediments and opportunities of our social and material worlds, connecting with many of the themes revealed in this project's research. From both standpoint and viewpoint theories, I constructed the term "standpoints" to draw lightly from these combined paradigms, leading to a definition of leadership that incorporates and expands their features.

Having identified current gaps in nonprofit leadership development (and with the leadership literature and many nonprofit leadership development programs in mind), leadership standpoints derive from the following eleven themes. These themes are divided into the primary, secondary, and tertiary dimensions that arose from the weight accorded to each throughout the data. Each theme combines the core verbs (describing and prescribing leadership actions) and adjectives (describing and prescribing leadership characteristics) that emerged:

Primary Dimension: Inclusion

- Forwarding Community and Diversity: Inclusive and Collaborative
- Distributing from the Center: Positional and Multidirectional
- Leading from the Heart: Socially and Ecologically Compassionate

Secondary Dimension: Performance

- Stretching toward a Higher Place: Brave and Visionary
- Inspiring Confidence: Intentional and Responsive
- Creating an Appetite and Opportunities for Continuous Learning: Curious, Generative, and Teachable
- Taking Care of Oneself: Fueled and Well

---

[11] The choreographer Mary Overlie was the first to use these terms, as cited in Hunter (n.d.: para. 3). Bogart and Landau (2005) expanded these six original viewpoints to the physical viewpoints of spatial relationship, kinesthetic response, shape, gesture, repetition, architecture, tempo, duration, and topography, and the vocal viewpoints of pitch, dynamic, acceleration/deceleration, silence, and timbre (Hunter n.d.: paras. 6–7).

Tertiary Dimension: Range

- Communicating through Effective Processes: Energetic and Eclectic
- Applying Polymathic Knowledge: Expert and Cross-Disciplinary
- Seeking and Advancing Peer Support: Networked and Upwardly Mobile
- Anchoring Values with Idiosyncratic Styles: Stable and Lithe

A theory of leadership standpoints manifests in each of these themes. For example, the first theme in the primary dimension about forwarding community and diversity through leadership that's inclusive and collaborative implicitly asserts that leaders should think and act from the many positions that can build unity, while working well with positions of difference. Moving down to a theme in the tertiary dimension such as applying polymathic knowledge, which urges leaders to be both expert and cross-disciplinary, leadership standpoints again provide a thesis for working with information that builds on one's strengths, while stretching to new knowledge standpoints outside of one's comfort zone.

The placing of inclusion first signifies much. In particular, the United States is at an inflection point regarding gender, race, and similar variables, and without full inclusion society will fail to maximize its talents and organizations of all types will lose legitimacy. That this dimension emerged so prominently in this project's data – and connects so firmly with calls from vast, cross-disciplinary literatures – warrants both attention and change.[12]

Using computer-aided techniques, an additional analysis of statistical patterns in the discourse about leadership from data collected in this project revealed five clusters connected to the eleven themes that further focus a language for nonprofit leadership. This analysis found that the next generation of nonprofit leaders should be anti-authoritarian to the core; set a vision for leadership as positive and forward-looking; think about leadership as a highly compassionate, reflective endeavor; emphasize both diversity and community; and use uncommon, simple, value-laden constructions that, in general, express a new and different kind of leadership than many people have inherited or channel in current practice.[13] To provide readers with glimpses of leadership standpoints in action, let's look at two examples that each focus some dimensions and corresponding themes.

---

[12] One example is "participative management" (Rolková & Viera Farkašová 2015). Another is a paradigm shifting, listening-based approach to leadership grounded in "multi-stakeholder dialogues" and "deliberative forms of engagement," as models that center human, relational approaches to all aspects of management ethics, while "fight[ing] indifference towards their neglect" (Bardy 2018: 2, 188, 56).

[13] A presentation of this computer-aided textual analysis was beyond this Element's scope. For an analysis of these post hoc results, please email don.waisanen@baruch.cuny.edu.

2.2 Two Brief Examples

2.2.1 A Board in Crisis

Darren is having a difficult time with his board. As the executive director of a small nonprofit that runs after-school programs for young people in a school district undergoing funding cuts in recent years, his program staff have opened up opportunities for artistic performances that would never have existed for scores of youth in the region. It has been a lifeline to improving their education, well-being, and, for many, future career options. Yet, with the loss of two foundation grants that supported 75 percent of the nonprofit's income during its first five years, this could be the organization's final quarter.[14] At yesterday night's board meeting, when he asked for everyone's input on what to do next, Darren observed that two dominant board members (one a powerful attorney, the other a prominent hedge fund manager), who are always the first to speak up among the eight present, said that they would write personal checks to keep the nonprofit afloat for one more quarter but that at the next meeting everyone may need to vote for the nonprofit's dissolution. All the other board members, who looked pressed for time and were busy checking their phones, nodded in agreement.

With leadership standpoints, Darren realized that he had let certain norms of apathy and closure develop among the group to this point. Over the past five years, most of the board had never volunteered for any events, did little fundraising, and often missed important meetings. Although the board was diverse, not everyone was included and engaged and, most important, the voices of those actually served were never present at these critical events. The lack of idea generation in favor of the quickest "let's just write a check and ride it out" approach was especially frustrating at this juncture. Darren understood that he had failed to distribute from the center, operating in positional and multidirectional ways – meaning that his focus had to switch to where people (including himself) positioned themselves relative to others, with an ability to shift that location in multiple ways. At base, many standpoints were missing, including other board members and program staff. To better address the funding crisis, Darren decided to apply leadership standpoints by calling an emergency board meeting with some big differences the next week.

First, he decided to cede control and rotate leadership by asking two board members who seldom spoke up to form an agenda for and facilitate the meeting, with a few areas of oversight that would further distribute power among the stakeholders. Second, each would bring one friend in a professional space

---

[14] I constructed both examples in this section as composites of several real-life challenges I have observed in teaching, consulting, and volunteering with many nonprofit organizations.

outside of any area that current board members worked in to the meeting (to broaden the range of ideas and positions present, tap into polymathic knowledge, and invite board expansion). Third, to reduce the distance between leaders and followers and broaden the standpoints at play, Darren would bring three young people served by the program to both share their experiences and act as a council and counsel for all ideas. Two program staff would also be present from here forward. Fourth, in preparation a survey would be distributed to all attending in advance, using a new meeting process and crowdsourcing platform (underscoring the tertiary dimension focusing on range and the theme of communicating through effective, energetic, and eclectic processes) requiring everyone to bring four distinct ideas to the table. All ideas would be put on a white board at the meeting and, for the first half hour, all thoughts about how to tackle the funding crisis, no matter how radical, would be entertained in randomized, paired conversations among the sixteen present, with a period of group critique and sifting after. Ranked-choice voting would be used to order areas for action across the following three months.[15]

As a result, Darren, the board, and the other stakeholders distilled the suggested actions down to a number of new initiatives. One would be to ditch the annual spring gala, which had always required too much in the way of overhead to make much of a dent in the nonprofit's financial picture. The board realized through this process that the nonprofit was too busy imitating other nonprofits having galas and had never asked the question of whether it was a good revenue generator to begin with. Everyone in the group made a written commitment to engage with two people offline and two people online with pitches for donations and to make themselves accountable for reporting the results at each meeting. Only one month into this new plan, the nonprofit hit its quarterly goals. The group made these changes permanent features of future meetings, especially through rotating facilitation where all would be truly involved.

Overall, Darren created new standpoints by attending to both who was at the table and how they were at the table. Attending to leadership standpoints gave a frame of reference for leadership knowledge, cultivated democratic attitudes, and offered the skills of broadly informed, effective idea generation and selection for the nonprofit's pressing challenge.

2.2.2 Breaking Through an Outbreak

A second scenario takes place during the coronavirus pandemic that affected nearly every person and organization on this planet. Kiara was just promoted to

---

[15] See "Ranked-choice voting (RCV)," Ballotpedia, https://ballotpedia.org/Ranked-choice_vot ing_(RCV).

a mid-level management position in a nonprofit shelter for women that serves a thousand clients every day, with some hundred staff. She now has ten direct reports, all frontline workers registering women facing homelessness or domestic abuse. Her staff provide meals and accommodation for their clients and help them find opportunities to transition to new employment and housing. With the COVID-19 outbreak, the state rightly deemed the shelter an essential business, but a thicket of issues immediately presented themselves: how to enforce social distancing and safety precautions in what's normally a crowded environment, as well as a facemask shortage that begs the question of whether available masks should go to clients, frontline workers, or senior leadership. Kiara wonders how she can best lead during this situation, especially since she's not on the executive team.

Kiara decides that there's two leadership standpoints she can immediately implement. The first involves leading from the heart with social and ecological compassion. She realizes that one advantage of her position is that she gets to see a lot of on-the-ground developments (the institution's ecology) in ways that the executive team may not. After the executive director mandates that all frontline workers come in during their regular work hours, she emails the executive team with a plea to expand their current standpoints and create a more inclusive policy – the pandemic has made school and childcare unavailable for many frontline workers, so any sense of normal work routines needs amending. She asks that all frontline workers be allowed to propose preferred work schedules and that conversations at least be started at all levels about how employees with children can navigate the current scenario. With this input, the executive team works out a new, staggered schedule across each twenty-four-hour period that allows for the maximum amount of clients to be served but with a greater use of evening shifts and hours that can align with family commitments and limited daycare possibilities for essential workers.

Second, Kiara applies the theme of taking care of oneself (and the need to be fueled and well) to advocate that she and her team simply cannot meet adequate levels of performance without some time out for rest, healthy eating, and exercise. Looking to how this standpoint affects everyone, self-care can be the first item to go in an emergency situation. However, Kiara pushes forward by carrying out one-on-one meetings with clients, frontline staff, and the executive team to generate ideas about what people most feel they need for their mental and physical health during all this hardship. Operating from these expanded standpoints leads Kiara to propose three radical actions: that a series of three computers for ordering up to $50 of food per day be made available to every person and client within the organization (using government stimulus money just received); that a local CrossFit instructor be hired to create daily videos for their organization, leading everyone through thirty-minute workouts via their phones or iPads; and that a special knitting station be set up at the shelter with materials garnered at the local Target, so that a space for taking time out is available – and might simultaneously address the mask shortage. Although these measures didn't make the situation any less painful, after two weeks of implementation Kiara notices that more people look visibly brighter, upbeat, and ready to tackle the enormity of the challenges with which they all are confronted. None of this would have been possible without Kiara's commitment to practicing inclusion, building spaces for performance, and thinking and acting with range.

2.3 Connections

Leadership standpoints build on a wealth of scholarly and practitioner literatures on leadership. For instance, Kanter's (2011) ideas about the need for leaders to "Zoom in," where they can "get a close look at select details – perhaps too close to make sense of them," and "Zoom out," where they can "see the big picture – but perhaps miss some subtleties and nuances," share affinities with the ability to position oneself in different spaces inherent in leadership standpoints. As Kanter expresses, "Both perspectives – worm's-eye and bird's-eye – have virtues and pathologies. *But they should be vantage points, not fixed positions. Leaders need multiple perspectives to get a complete picture*" (paras. 3-4; emphasis added).[16]

Given the world's present volatility and how "the most consequential and devastating risks are the risks of bad leadership," in particular, "leaders and organizations that do not amplify their lens to incorporate the views, risks and opportunities and consequences of ignoring (or even damaging) their full spectrum of key stakeholders ... run the risk of losing to competitors, engaging in misadventures, increasing reputation risk, liabilities and losses or even losing their license to operate" (Bonime-Blanc 2020: 42, 25). As skills for leaders to cultivate, all involve broad analysis, movement, and practiced shifts through one's and others' positionalities.

Leadership standpoints also fit with big-picture calls to evolve societies upward through integrative, flexible, complex, and global "new modes of being," or structures of thinking founded on an "open system of values with an infinite number of modes of living available to us" (Beck & Cowan 2006: 39, 29). They similarly promote forms of leadership that "roam over vast mindscapes seeing patterns and connections others do not notice," while "interact[ing] comfortably with many conceptual worlds" to constantly survey "the whole while tinkering

---

[16] These concepts are similar to the leadership metaphors of being on both the "balcony" and the "dance floor" provided in Heifetz, Grashow, and Linsky (2009: 7).

expertly with the parts" (110, 107). At their core, leadership standpoints are deliberative, future-oriented, and practical in spirit.

Leadership standpoints further connect with the idea of "stretching" in leadership and human development. For instance, the "productive zone of disequilibrium" pits leadership challenges against the status quo, urging leaders to keep teams focused on the difficult, collective adaptive work that people in an organization will try to avoid given the personal losses at stake (Heifetz, Grashow, & Linsky 2009; Waisanen 2021). Lev Vygotsky's parallel concept of the "Zone of Proximal Development," or the creation of spaces where human growth best takes place, with conscious attention to setting the norms and conditions where people are motivated to perform beyond their present abilities (Holzman 2017: 27–28, 51), additionally undergirds the type of stretching critical to leadership standpoints. Work on body intelligence and how people use space – all important for leaders' awareness about consciously communicating – further fits with contemporary approaches to positive leadership (e.g. Buller 2013). This Element incorporates and adds to these ideas by providing expanded insights and practices for nonprofit leaders. The next section will provide a deeper look at these relevant connections.

2.4 Scope

In this Element, I focus on the applications of leadership standpoints to nonprofit practice. This isn't to limit their use in other spheres such as corporate leadership workshops, government agency programs, and more. These spaces need the type of leaders and leadership development described in these pages. Yet, given how leadership standpoints grew out of a look at nonprofit leadership development programs and data of all kinds from across the NYCTLF (and particularly through alumni interviews),[17] both for scope and to support this Element's claims, attention will be placed exclusively on nonprofit situations and examples.[18]

While certainly applicable to many of these issues, I would also refer readers to works such as *The Jossey-Bass Handbook of Nonprofit Leadership and*

---

[17] These interviews also follow calls in the literature for "more research attention . . . to the wisdom, creativity, and insight of leaders of voluntary organizations, focusing on their theories-in-use, which they use to create the meaning of their own and others' experience and action" (Kay 1994: 285).

[18] This raises a question about whether leadership standpoints could be suited to a leadership context that seems at opposites. For example, it might be hard to imagine their use in military leadership training, with its associations of hierarchy and subservience to chains of command. This is partly good reason to tie leadership standpoints to the sector from which they emanated. Then again, see the remarkably adaptive, lithe, and ecologically focused military strategies of Paul Van Riper described in Gladwell (2005: 99–146).

Management for a sweeping overview of the more granular historical, legal and political, financial, contractual, staffing and compensation, and board governance aspects of nonprofit leadership. As the handbook makes clear, "one of the most exciting aspects of studying nonprofit management today is that experts are still trying to grapple with what it is, how it acts, and what it will be" (Never 2016: 81).[19] Leadership standpoints build on this plea.

Following research on human development, leadership standpoints involve skills to be practiced and characteristics to be cultivated (see Lilienfeld et al. 2015). They provide a practical framework for use in leadership development programs and leadership in action but aren't meant to be universalized. If there's anything leadership standpoints underscore, it's that putting fixed boundaries around a theory of leadership would stand at odds with the continuous updating and potential for additional standpoints to inform leadership.

Moreover, while much of this Element focuses on what happens within organizations, organizations are open systems that interpret, adapt, and respond to environmental change (see Katz & Kahn 1978; Weick & Sutcliffe 2015).[20] In the following sections, readers can thus assume that anything being written about leadership also applies both within and without. For instance, applying an expert and cross-disciplinary focus within an organization will inevitably arise from an openness to outside learnings. As another example, every message a leader sends externally is also heard by stakeholders within an organization. Nonprofit organizations are open, evolving systems with porous boundaries.

In the following sections, I first examine some of the relevant literature supporting this Element. I then turn to an examination of other leadership development programs, comparing and contrasting a snapshot sample of what's happening in this space to show how the theory of leadership standpoints works with extant fields of practice. Next, I dive into details on each of the dimensions and themes. Each of these approaches builds a base of evidence and practices for a theory of leadership standpoints.

Finally, I distill several implications from this project for the future of nonprofit leadership theory and development. My hope is that this Element provides a space for nonprofit professionals to reflect on the state of their practices, lifting themselves and others up in that process.

---

[19] To not overstate generalizability, I position leadership standpoints with what Renz and Herman (2016: 283) call "promising practices" for nonprofit leadership.

[20] The long-standing PESTLE (political, economic, sociocultural, technological, legal, and environmental) tool that many in the business world use for scanning external contexts is based on the same assumptions about open systems. See "PEST analysis," MindTools, www.mindtools.com/pages/article/newTMC_09.htm.

From another angle, I'd advise readers to consider the following question as you explore leadership standpoints: What if we don't implement this type of leadership? I urge you to consider what kinds of leadership we have seen, both historical and contemporary, that form as opposites to the verbs and nouns at play in the framework. A colleague reminded me of a scene from the movie *Whiplash*, where the actor J. K. Simmons, playing a bandleader, berates a young apprentice to the point of meltdown, illustrating the horrors of certain kinds of leadership.[21] While many of us may never have experienced that extreme, I'm sure that everyone reading this Element can identify with experiences with less than desirable leadership. These provide a good foil for what's to come. For further context, let's next look to a few relevant ideas from leadership research.

3 A Brief Overview of Relevant Ideas about Leadership

In my years of working with professionals in the nonprofit sector, there's a question I like to pose at the outset of any leadership training: If you were suddenly promoted to a position of leadership and wanted to find out as much as you could about the topic, what do you think you would discover? Participants' responses to this question typically range from any number of ideas they've heard about in a past class (e.g. "situational leadership") to inchoate ruminations picked up from popular culture or work experiences (e.g. "leaders need to show unwavering commitment").

I like to introduce the idea that whatever they currently believe about leadership didn't occur in a vacuum; that to have more choices in one's leadership practices it's critical to move from narrow, unexamined personal theories to broadly informed public ideas; and that there's a vast body of knowledge to draw from in conceptualizing what leadership is and should be. In this regard, to understand how leadership standpoints work and the possibilities that they offer nonprofit professionals, it's critical to look at the relevant literature.

There is no shortage of attention to leadership. In 2021, a Google search for the term "leadership" listed approximately 6,490,000,000 results, while a Google Scholar search of the same term listed approximately 4,640,000 studies of the subject.[22] Amid all this work on the topic, a number of prominent scholarly and practitioner theories of leadership have risen, fallen, or continued to receive traction across a variety of sectors. Foremost among them are trait theories that "emphasize the physical and psychological characteristics of

---

[21] "Not quite my tempo: Whiplash (2014)," YouTube, December 19, 2016, www.youtube.com /watch?v=GBvBu5ErSSo.

[22] A search of "nonprofit leadership" in Google Scholar also listed approximately 492,000 results.

individual actors," behavioral theories that "focus on the actions that set a leader apart from others," and situational theories that "attempt to capture the specific characteristics of a scenario, including those that pertain to the followers or subordinates and the context in which the situation occurs" (Golensky & Hager 2020: 55–56). While a complete examination of past and present leadership literatures is beyond this Element's scope, a number of ideas are most germane to leadership standpoints as a framework.

3.1 Diversity and Distribution

More than ever, leadership studies center on the influence of culture, diverse contexts, and the many ways that leaders can exert power. Drawing from multicultural and transformative leadership studies, "socially conscious leadership" exemplifies how "the solutions that our world needs must be rooted in collaborative leadership that honors individual empowerment, community building, and social justice" (Arora, Elawar, & Cheng 2019: 38). "Sustainability leadership" similarly follows the UN Brundtland Commission's definition in its formulation of leadership: "Meeting the needs of the present generation without compromising the ability of future generations to meet their own needs" (Way, 2012: para. 1; Hargreaves & Fink 2012).[23] Of note, these definitions highlight that a leader's responsibility is not simply to serve their own institution but to steward people and resources wisely beyond it.

With relevance to leadership standpoints, constructionist, feminist, and similar paradigms undergird much of this work (see Ospina & Sorenson 2006). Some reasons are clear. Although women comprise nearly three-quarters of nonprofit employees in the United States, they hold less than half of the sector's CEO positions and make an average of two-thirds the salary of their counterparts in equivalent leadership roles.[24] Women of color hold less than 14 percent of nonprofit board memberships nationwide (The White House Project 2009; Mook 2019). Although the gender gap is narrowing in certain nonprofit job categories (e.g. human resources, operations, and public relations), the simultaneous overrepresentation of women in the sector as a whole and underrepresentation of women in top positions highlight a continuing need for improvements in nonprofit leadership.

---

[23] The Iroquois have a precept that every decision must be made in terms of the seventh generation to come. See "What is the seventh generation principle?," Indigenous Corporate Training blog, May 30, 2012, www.ictinc.ca/blog/seventh-generation-principle.

[24] See "Gender equity in nonprofits has a way to go," *The Nonprofit Times*, March 5, 2018, www .thenonprofittimes.com/npt_articles/gender-equity-nonprofits-way-go/.

Following the work of Herminia Ibarra, traditional divisions of labor can also create gendered leadership practices (Kanter 2011: para. 27),[25] although women tend to be better evaluated in the areas of empathy and communication, which are critical for leading team-based organizations in the modern workplace (Appelbaum, Audet, & Miller 2003). Whereas early theories of leadership extolled traditionally masculine characteristics, modern conceptions of leadership effectiveness align more with feminine styles. Research suggests that employees view leaders practicing feminine styles more favorably than masculine styles in the areas of motivation, creativity, problem-solving, and other key skills associated with transformational leadership (Eagly & Carli 2003).[26] While gender is a far more fluid construct than the language of such work represents (i.e. there's a too easy slippage between sex and gender markers – and more research is needed beyond the feminine/masculine binary),[27] they at least offer a window into continuing projects demonstrating the many different standpoints from which leaders can operate.

Leadership grounded in diversity has also been extended through "*worldly* leadership" that, as Case, Turnbull, and Khakwani (2012: 3) note, beckons

> a pooling of the combined leadership wisdoms from all parts of the globe – whether these are contemporary or ancient wisdoms. We fear that as the world becomes increasingly homogenous as a result of the "flattening" impact of the internet and advancing global communication technology, the existing dominant voices may drive out the leadership wisdoms of minority, indigenous and ancient wisdoms. It does not have to be so. With ... new technologies, an opportunity now presents itself for leaders across the world to share and combine the leadership knowledge and practice that exist in many corners of the world: wisdoms that would otherwise remain unknown outside their community.

Each of these approaches invites expansive theories of leadership. Regardless of the focus, they all call for tapping into many voices, especially from marginalized communities, which are critical to future work in this area (Schenker & Perry 2005).

---

[25] Further focusing on how leadership cannot be culture- and gender-neutral, Ayman and Korabik (2010: 157) describe some factors making up the "labyrinth" that women and other leaders face: "stereotypes and schemes, ingroup-outgroup dynamics, role expectations, power and status differentials, and differential attributions made about and rewards given for similar behavior." Rosener (1990: paras. 6–8) also argues that masculine styles tend to be grounded in "transactional leadership," whereas feminine styles tend to be more oriented toward "transformational" and "interactive leadership."

[26] Elevating women to positions of leadership can have a powerful multiplier effect (Duke 2017).

[27] Although there's a lot of linguistic slippage about sex and gender in leadership research, where possible here I follow the preference in much scholarship for using a "feminine style" as a non-essentialist, gendered performance (see Dow & Tonn 1993).

One related focus in current literatures on leadership development involves networked leadership. Comparing and summarizing traditional conceptions of leadership against newer ideas about the networked leader, Grant, Scearce, and Flower (2010: 74) find that the former emphasizes one's position and authority, directive styles, transactional relationships, individuals and control, and generally top-down forms of command. In contrast, the latter type of leader emphasizes roles and behaviors, collective and facilitative approaches, emergent processes, relationships and connections, and bottom-up forms of command. Networked approaches advance a distributed and inclusive form of leadership, connecting with how people now orient themselves to everyday life. In a world where smartphones and social media build one-to-one communication between people on a mass level (Fogg 2008), we are, in a very real sense, living our lives in networks.

Leadership theories that fail to account for this groundbreaking shift away from closed to more open-ended organizational models, and the demands for transparency and interactivity that they generate, risk missing a key aspect of how leadership works in this era. There is still much to process on this horizon, including how no single unifying theory of leadership exists – or probably should exist given the literature's turn to diversity and distribution.[28]

3.2 Working with Leadership Paradoxes

For this Element's purposes, one paradoxical result of having so many different ideas and practices about leadership is a haziness about what exactly people are trying to pin down. Too often, "there is no common understanding of what people mean by the term or how its value is demonstrated in practice."[29] At the same time, many definitions of leadership abound. De Pree (2004: xxii) says that leadership is "liberating people to do what is required of them in the most effective and humane way possible." Bennis argues that "leadership is the capacity to translate vision into reality," while Joanne Ciulla finds that "leadership is not a person or a position. It is a complex moral relationship between people, based on trust, obligation, commitment, emotion, and a shared vision of the good" (Daskal 2016). McCauley, Van Velsor, and Ruderman (2010: 2) even summarize "leadership roles and processes as those that facilitate setting direction, creating alignment, and maintaining commitment in groups of people who share common work."

---

[28] There are many more theories of leadership that could be described in this section, but for the sake of scope I refer readers to Grint's (2010) excellent overview of other theories.

[29] "Leadership and development: Paper 2 in PSJP's defining key concepts series," Philanthropy for Social Justice and Peace, March 2019: 2, www.psjp.org/wp-content/uploads/2019/03/Leadership-and-Development-March-2019.pdf.

Additionally, many classic, new, and off-the-shelf schemes and models have been used in leadership development. Some programs are driven by DiSC®, 360-degree feedback tools, or the Belbin team roles,[30] while others focus on everything from a certain theoretically derived approach (e.g. transformational leadership) to simply relaying one's personal stories of leadership and lessons learned. Leadership is viewed as either an end in itself or a means to an end, but creating sharper details for developing leaders is too often hindered by a lack of funding or wanting money to go to a program rather than building organizational infrastructure (McCauley, Van Velsor, & Ruderman 2010: 14–15).

That so much thought and practice has been devoted to leadership begs a question: Why not just choose from an existing theory of leadership for nonprofit leadership programs like the NYCTLF? First, there's no need to leave this work behind; some of the best ideas about leadership can and should be integrated into such a framework. Yet, second, to develop a context-sensitive theory that addresses the needs and interests of nonprofit professionals, who increasingly represent diverse backgrounds, requires a deeper test of what should be included and what's missing in contemporary nonprofit leadership development.

For instance, in a recent report, the *Changing Leadership Dynamics in Nonprofit Organizations*, the authors highlighted how financial management, mission and program passion, a willingness to fundraise, the management of a diverse workforce, an appetite for growing the organization's talent, a willingness to collaborate with board members, being savvy with media and technology, and an "Intelligence and Thoughtfulness When Projecting a World View that Embraces New Ideas" will be critical to the next generation of leaders (Oppenheim 2017: 11–13). Overall, such sources assert the many factors at work in modern nonprofit life, from leading and managing organizational change to staying abreast of developments in interdisciplinary fields of practice. With this backdrop for leadership standpoints in mind, let's look at other nonprofit leadership development programs for further insight into relevant theory and practice.

3.3 A Brief Look at Nonprofit Leadership Programs

Some sense of what other, similar programs have been doing in this space was helpful in developing leadership standpoints. The New York metropolitan area is home to 13,000 nonprofit organizations with more than 660,000 employees (DiNapoli 2019: 11). There appear to be more than 100 nonprofit leadership

---

[30] See, for instance, the websites for DiSC® (www.discprofile.com/what-is-disc/overview/) and Belbin (www.belbin.com/about/belbin-team-roles/).

programs offered in the New York metropolitan area alone, ranging from professional certificate programs at universities to local fellowships, peer coaching, and mentoring programs as well as an array of one-off workshops and seminars.

We reviewed a snowball sample of available materials on these nonprofit leadership programs (through their websites, links, etc.) to get a sense of what's unique and common between them. Although these programs vary widely in length, scope, and format, they tend to share a topline emphasis on management best practices and developing tools to confront the challenges posed by limited funding, recruitment and retention, and maintaining organizational performance. They also share a concern for collaborative learning, coaching, building community power, listening and storytelling, an attentiveness to diverse histories, and expanding toward more equitable futures for all.

Many nonprofit leadership programs are geared toward senior and executive-level leaders, while others target emerging leaders. Programs focused on senior leadership often emphasize strategic management, developing mission priorities, and setting direction for nonprofits. Emerging leaders' programs tend to stress guiding principles of social justice and a need to cultivate new cohorts of nonprofit leaders who reflect the rapidly changing demographics of the United States. Many programs highlight the importance of building social capital. As one program evaluation found: "In an era where one of the most prevalent issues being surfaced by leaders is increasing fragmentation, narrow focus, and isolation, these convenings offer an opportunity to build relationships and promote exchange, thus addressing one of the most important leadership needs" (DeVelde et al. 2005: 2).

Several programs stood out as noteworthy relative to the NYCTLF's mission. One fellowship cultivating "high-potential emerging leaders" is the Institute for Nonprofit Practice's Community Fellows Program, which recently expanded to the New York metropolitan area. This six-month program assembles participants once a month to explore topics in community organizing, personal brand building, fundraising, networking, and "developing your leadership narrative."[31] The program is fully funded for a cohort of twenty fellows and results in a Certificate in Community Leadership and Social Change. The program's recruitment materials highlight its emphasis on social justice and its mission to build a network of "change leaders" in the nonprofit sector.

---

[31] "Community fellows program," Institute for Nonprofit Practice. www.nonprofitpractice.org /community-fellows-program.

Another notable New York–based resource for nonprofit leaders is the Community Resource Exchange (CRE), a consulting firm that, for more than forty years, has offered customized support, peer training, and executive coaching to nonprofit professionals. CRE's flagship program is a seven-month leadership caucus for senior leaders focused on organizational decision-making and management, funded in partnership with New York City's Department of Youth and Community Development.[32] As part of their progression with CRE, "Participants reported that they learned by doing, tried new behaviors, and received reinforcement and feedback from peers within the caucus. Peer networks emerged naturally because of shared experience in a safe, facilitated setting. Participants cited connection with others as an antidote to feelings of isolation in their leadership roles" (Lobell, Sikka, & Sauvage-Mar 2009). CRE's method seeks to accommodate a range of learning styles, promote peer-based learning, and create a reflective learning space for participants, using multiple learning methods to have an impact on leadership development (Lobell, Sikka, & Sauvage-Mar 2009).

Outside of New York, organizations such as the Rockwood Leadership Institute lead similar training programs across the country. Rockwood's leadership programs reflect its stated commitment to "radical inclusion" by welcoming participants at all levels of organizational leadership (Nipper 2019). It's worth diving into some of the institute's details at length, as they offer a noteworthy perspective:

> The dominant paradigm often focuses on providing individuals with knowledge and skills to increase their capacity to move into leadership roles. Leadership programs that take a deficit approach to leadership, supplying the missing skills or tools, often run the risk of reinforcing power dynamics that privilege external expertise and solutions that fail to address the structural ways in which power and privilege are perpetuated. It is important that leadership approaches build on community based power with a framework for understanding and tackling the institutionalized causes of economic disparities that show up along lines of race. ... Many people of color interviewed ... explained that their leadership is rendered invisible when they do not conform to the dominant leadership norms that privilege a directive style of leadership even when they are actually accomplishing more through a facilitative style that unleashes team capacity ... The leadership values of love, equity, justice, and community, which are critical to leadership success for people of color, are often not supported within the dominant leadership models. The privileging of a model aligned with the dominant culture perpetuates internalized oppression, discrimination and

---

[32] "Leadership development – CRE," Community Resource Exchange (CRE), www.crenyc.org /services/leadership-development/.

white privilege. As a result, people of color will not have influence at policy tables, in designing community based solutions, and in addressing disparities along a number of political and socio-economic dimensions. (Perry, Meehan, & Reinalt 2009: 6, 4)

Integral to addressing these issues are the skills and perspectives of community determination, focusing on assets rather than deficits, and experience-driven and relational criteria (6). To use "approaches that build the capacity of individuals and communities to deal with the impact of internalized oppression and prejudice, and a history of racial trauma," listening, storytelling, inner healing, facilitation and convening skills, as well as community coaching are all components of Rockwood's programming (7–9). To address structural racism, a social justice framework, place-based leadership strategies, policy, advocacy, and organizing skills, as well as novel ideas such as compensating participation and providing mini-grants can all be used (9–11).

This project drew further inspiration from the approaches of CompassPoint, a five-decades-old national nonprofit based in northern California that sees leadership development as a means for advancing social justice. CompassPoint spotlights how "Our communities demand and deserve an approach to leadership development that centers liberation: one that nurtures people and relationships, lives at the crossroads of our urgent day-to-day needs and a visionary narrative of the future, and one that understands how our different struggles are bound up together" (Cubías n.d.: para. 9, emphasis in original removed). Modeling this type of leadership,

> we didn't want to re-create a strategy process where a team of powerful people disappears behind closed doors to emerge with a vision and mandate that gets handed down to everyone else. Instead, we saw our role as sourcing strategy up from our own roots; *codifying the values that were already there and giving voice to aspirations about what we need to be together.* (para. 13, emphasis added)

Note how critical it is to both create change and tap into individual and collective values with histories as a starting point. The metaphor of "roots" implies that this work has a basis, can be defined, and should be connected to a moral vision.

At the same time, some traditional classroom-format leadership training programs are worth highlighting. For example, Columbia University Business School's Developing Leaders Program targets "high potential nonprofit managers" and seeks to build participants' skills in negotiation while bolstering managerial effectiveness. The intensive six-day program costs $5,950 and results in a certificate. The school's corresponding program for senior nonprofit leaders touts its four week, twenty-day, module-based format as an opportunity for participants to integrate management theory and practice while building their network, at a cost of $11,250.[33] I'm including this price comparison only to show that nonprofit leadership programs vary widely not only in length, format, and focus but also in their degree of accessibility. In New York City, where nonprofit employees make an average annual salary of just over $60,000 (DiNapoli 2019: 7), some nonprofit leadership programs may simply be out of reach for those without significant means or substantial tuition assistance.

Compared to such programs, the NYCT underwrites the entire cost of the NYCTLF to make the program as accessible as possible for nonprofit practitioners. From the program's inception, there has been no bachelor's degree requirement for admission either. Removing these types of barriers constitutes core values for the program, signaling that nonprofit leadership development should be inclusive and equitable, reaching both horizontally and vertically across the sector to improve participants' capacities. The program is open to a broad cross-section of the nonprofit sector and organizations in many fields (e.g. community development, youth empowerment, arts and culture, health, etc.).

Overall, this snapshot of nonprofit leadership development highlights differences not only between programs but also clusters of aligned theory and practice. One substantial concern across many of these programs is the established "nonprofit racial leadership gap" and social justice–related themes.[34] Another is that leadership should extend beyond the formalities of organizational charts to be put within the reach of diverse people.

Parallel to nonprofits' needs, the government sector has been facing similar challenges in its leadership development efforts. In general, "there is an absence of an agreed upon model for agency-based leadership development programs," which have taken a "let 'a thousand flowers bloom'" approach to the issue (Abner et al. 2019: 11). In other words, definition-less leadership is largely the norm in government leadership training and development, begging more coherence around what this work is and can accomplish.

This project doesn't seek to provide an inflexible definition of nonprofit leadership but rather questions what happens when we don't have a lithe, contextually sensitive vision for leadership – that's always open to further development – with accessible, memorable, and actionable features and

---

[33] Senior leaders program for nonprofit professionals, Columbia Business School, www8 .gsb.columbia.edu/execed/program-pages/details/118/SLP.

[34] This gap has been well established in research. See *Race to Lead: Confronting the Nonprofit Racial Leadership Gap*, Building Movement Project report, 2017, https://racetolead.org/wp-content/uploads/2017/12/RacetoLead_ExecutiveSummary-2.pdf.

functions to guide practice. Since budgets figure prominently in decisions to dedicate oneself or one's time to leadership development, there are also implications for costs, as it's easier to build from defined programs or others' learnings than to start from scratch in every new effort. To get us further down this path, let's now explore leadership standpoints' dimensions and themes.

4 The Primary Dimension: Inclusion

Seeking to contribute to the nonprofit field, the remainder of this Element details what a twenty-first-century leadership theory for the growing number of nonprofit professional development programs could use in whole or part. Toward this end, in-depth interviews were carried out with a random sample of NYCTLF alumni to understand their post-program understanding of leadership and what kind of framework could best meet the aspirations of nonprofit professionals in New York City and beyond.[35]

Working with the program's alumni meant that we were starting with people who had been through a leadership training program and had carved out time in their lives to think about leadership ideas and practices. They also brought backgrounds, experiences, and stories outside of it to their understandings of leadership. We sought to interview practitioners doing the day-to-day work of nonprofits to capture what's practical, what's not, and – since the NYCTLF is a fellowship for "emerging leaders" – what the next generation of nonprofit practitioners could tell us that they need. Putting their voices into this project was itself an important positional move, elevating those served rather than service providers as a focal point for developing the dimensions and themes.

On top of extensive leadership literature reviews, program comparisons, and the wealth of data available via the NYCTLF, including five years of program materials, the data and results from the complete eighteen-month program evaluation, instructor lessons, and ongoing discussions with program staff, ten alumni of the NYCTLF program were interviewed as part of this study. These included eight females and two males.[36] Participants held a number of managerial and leadership roles within their respective organizations.[37] Position

---

[35] For access to the interview questions we used with all of our participants, please email don. waisanen@baruch.cuny.edu.

[36] The field of leadership development [LD] itself now calls for "frame-breaking LD research" working with "under or unrepresented, demographically diverse leaders," including "women and LD," "racial minorities and LD," and "LGBTQ+" leaders (Vogel et al. 2020: 13). The NYCTLF consciously invites participants with these identities into its work.

[37] Although the interviews weren't the only source for constructing the themes in this project (they stood atop data generated from the NYCTLF program across five years), recent scholarship is

titles ranged from program officer and project manager among entry and mid-level participants to chief operating officer, vice president, and executive director at the more senior end. The participants represented organizations of different ages and sizes, ranging from a 2-year-old educational nonprofit with a staff of 20, to a 40-year-old victims services nonprofit with 800 employees. These nonprofits also varied in their work and populations served. Two participants worked at the intersection of youth empowerment and sports, three worked in museum contexts, others worked in youth vocational training, public health advocacy, initiatives for women and girls, services for domestic abuse, and social services for seniors.

In what follows, I pursued a collaborative, reflexive research process that emerged from the themes themselves, thinking about my own positionality in these discussions while making the interviewees' phrasings and terms prominent throughout (see Alcoff 1991). After the interviews, I coded and abductively analyzed the interview transcripts (relative to the prior NYCTLF program data, the leadership literature, and other programs), looking for the "intensity and frequency" of key constructions and words,[38] before applying an additional computer-aided textual analysis to the participants' comments to explore, cluster, and prioritize specific themes that could inform a theory of leadership (Saldaña 2015).[39]

Since the interviews manifest many verbs having to do with leadership practices and adjectives describing normative characteristics, I labeled the themes with both verbs and adjectives in attempting to capture participants' ideas about this subject. Figure 3 provides an overview of all the themes. While each of the following sections analyzes the themes arising from the interviews,

---

clear about the sample size for these types of qualitative interviews. Many bring the inappropriate expectations and logic of statistical rather than qualitative analysis to such work. Yet ten is entirely suitable for a project "when the unit of analysis is the concept" (categories generated for a conceptual model, not a case, group, or person), where the richness of data is critical for saturating themes and since there is ultimately "no numerical formula for determining saturation" (Low 2019: 133, 135, 137). Increasingly, researchers have discovered that large sample sizes for this type of work "may make it difficult to examine data in all their complexity, limiting ability to probe data collection, develop emergent questions, or contextualize quotes" (Roy et al. 2015: 243–260). Moreover, "instead of relying on the number of times a concept emerges to convey its importance, theoretical saturation rests on close examination of all the contexts and related themes that are somehow related to it" (254). In a landmark study, Guest, Bunce, and Johnson (2006) set out to interview sixty participants and found that the main concepts all arose after only six interviews were analyzed, showing how "meaningful themes and useful interpretations" can arise in non-probabalistic samples of this size, particularly when there's a clear conceptual focus to the work (78).

[38] For more on this methodology, see Foss (2018: 413).

[39] As mentioned, I kept in mind the idea of theoretical "saturation," or the point at which the data pragmatically saturated into certain themes (not necessarily the point at which saturation is fully reached: a problematic notion). For more on this topic, see Saunders et al. (2018).

Figure 3 Leadership standpoints visualization

as much as possible participants' own language is used to provide agency and accuracy to their conceptions. The following constitute the main findings from these interviews, beginning with the primary dimension that focuses on non-profit leadership inclusion.

4.1 Forwarding Community and Diversity: Inclusive and Collaborative

If there's any theme that stuck out among the rich data offered in this project, it's that the next generation of nonprofit leaders will have to foster community and incorporate diversity, equity, and inclusion into all their thinking and actions; and that's truly the part that's unique: not just some of their thinking, but *all* of it. One participant related: "I think the fellowship is on track with the eclectic array of leadership that they provide . . . But I think if they're going to adopt one main [theory] . . . they just have to make sure that they don't lose the piece of the importance of diversity and inclusion in any leadership practice."[40] There may have been a time when these were peripheral considerations for leaders, but the fellows brought into unambiguous focus that such an era has passed. Advancing community and diversity must be at the center of contemporary nonprofit leadership.

The next generation of nonprofit leaders should foster both unity and diversity throughout their organizations. After presenting this project's findings to a variety of stakeholders for feedback, many found the emphasis on unity notable in the context of diversity. How the two concepts relate carries much meaning for nonprofit practice. One interviewee shared how "building a sense of community was very strong throughout the [NYCTLF] program, and that's a great model for leadership." Another said that "you need to have an ensemble ... That doesn't mean that everybody agrees all the time, but it does mean that there's a spirit of togetherness and collaboration." Each step of the way, community's importance stood out.

At the same time, a participant related that the experience of being in the room with so many different people during the fellowship performed its own lesson:

> The Fellowship had a wonderful emphasis on diversity, equity, and inclusion. It seems clear to me that that is key going forward, not only in terms of social consciousness, but also in terms of organizations being effective ... Everybody needs to practice it to be good at it. We are not going to have the best ideas in the room unless the room represents the world.

In essence, leaders who are consciously seeking to make sure their spaces represent the planet create whole and inclusive rather than partial and exclusive communities. Even when working on the most local of issues, the expectation is that leaders apply a global perspective to their efforts.

While not often thought about in this way, we heard repeatedly how attention to difference is its own leadership curriculum. One participated shared how "it's just so instructive to be surrounded by people from radically different walks of life, radically different cultures, class, all of it." Another fellow also noted how:

> The cultural diversity of the New York Community Trust [Fellowship] is a crucial facet of that program ... The social economic diversity of the people in the room, also felt really powerful and important to me. That feels like an important part of the curriculum, in addition to the concepts taught. Who's in the room is really important. I think they do a great job of being intentional

---

[40] For all interviewees' quotations in this Element, I have removed filler words such as "you know," "sort of," and "like" for easier reading.

about who that is. I don't think it can be separated out. I think that's also
a show of leadership, about who you feel it's important to bring into a space.

A first step to fostering community is to consider who is in the room (diversity).
Creating a space where everybody has an equal opportunity to share with one
another is seen as critical to that effort. One implication is that nonprofit
leadership development programs should do everything possible to model
ideals for leadership that stand in contrast to the less communal and diverse
ways that many organizational spaces operate.

Yet, to advance, nonprofit professionals will also have to care about the
practices that then take place. Being inclusive and collaborative was seen as
parallel to diversity and community: it's important to have diverse people at the
table, but it's also critical to collaborate with them so that these voices are then
acknowledged and incorporated into nonprofit work. The term "collaboration"
and variants such as "collective" and "empowering" came up many times across
the interviews. One participant clarified how this means cultivating and valuing
multiple perspectives. Empowering others requires give and take or, as one
person put it, asking questions and stating positions, but not in a disruptive
way. Emphasizing community and diversity further supported a distributional
premise that "anyone can step up in a way that they can become a person of
influence across an organization or a community."[41]

Without conscious implementation, these inclusive and collaborative values
will sit as unrealized organizational ideals that can easily become a source of
frustration or conflict. According to one interviewee, the fellowship went
against an idea that "if you work for a diverse organization, then you are
being inclusive. But it's more about what you do on a day to day [basis], little
decisions you make, that are going to make that change."[42] In all decision-
making, whether preparing for new hires or reading financial statements, the
fellowship alumni found applications of this lens critical to future nonprofit
leadership.

Anti-racism and a gender equality lens form the basis for challenging
inherited models of leadership that many saw as unreflectively channeled in
so much nonprofit practice. Almost every interviewee wanted staff presence and
follow-through brought to work on community and diversity. According to one

---

[41] This phrase also fits with much current literature, for example Cecchi-Dimeglio (2020).

[42] Much praise has been placed on "psychological safety," or the "shared belief held by members of
a team that the team is safe for interpersonal risk-taking," according to Amy Edmondson
(Duhigg 2016: para. 34; Edmondson 2019). The emphasis on community and diversity connects
with how safe, open, and vulnerable individuals feel that they can be in organizations. In another
sense, psychological safety is directly related to inclusion – who would feel included if they
didn't feel safe, after all?

participant, nonprofit leadership training programs should "double and triple down on their ... focus on what it means, on racial equity and anti-racist structures in nonprofits." Since the idea of participation has long been on leadership agendas (see Freire 1970), but people of color continue to be underrepresented in nonprofit leadership positions (Allard & Reuter n.d.), this theme presents a call to action. It takes a concerted effort to de-bias leadership. One participant said she "really appreciated some of the training that we got on diversity and gender, and making sure that I was being conscious of any bias that I might be bringing to my management." Many realized how they and others had been enacting biases with others, despite espoused commitments.

Overall, the need for shifting one's positions, lenses, and abilities in different directions – all characteristics of leadership standpoints – grounded interviewees' observations. One person said it's important "to be inclusive and to not project this white dominant culture in your hiring practices," in particular. Another shared, "the ways that hierarchy is within organizations are relics of a patriarchal white supremacist system and ... I think that's something that's missing out of leadership trainings." More effort should be put toward "the context of a lot of these roles within the framework of inequality or identity politics," with an "understanding of race and social power and that it's a responsibility of a leader to actively look for places where traditional power structures can be flipped" or "neutralized or named."

In a running refrain, participants were quick to note how easily inconsistencies could manifest in this area between organizational symbolism and on-the-ground actions, highlighting how inclusion means being at the table while collaboration represents the equity or follow-through in practical matters. One person noted,

> I see it also with how some leaders forget that their staff [are] also part of the community that they're serving ... So don't over here talk about pay equity and then over here be trying to negotiate people down to the lowest salary or allow there to be a large gap between what you pay your females and what you pay your males.

Paying attention to these issues means diagnosing, sometimes painfully, the systemic and long-standing habits present in organizational life. Developing anti-oppressive leadership means looking for contradictions and being willing to revise practices and policies to allow others to flourish.

In nonprofit leadership training programs, staff and instructors must exemplify community and diversity in their own projections too. This means that a leadership development experience should be more than just content delivery. One participant remarked about one of the program instructors: "I felt like he brought to the table a clear confidence in his own abilities as a facilitator and in the content area, but [was] also very intentional about making space for others and providing opportunities for peer learning as well, which I thought were all great qualities." The fellows wanted to see consistency across sessions in this regard. One person noted, "not everything was about diversity, inclusion. But every one session definitely took that lens at some point or another. And so I think every staff member really embodied that, which I thought was refreshing." Combining areas such as "servant leadership" or "leading from within," placing these in the context of what's happening in nonprofits, adding a racial equity lens, "and making it practical for what I could do on Monday" were seen as ideals. Translated to the world of leadership practice, one consequence is that nonprofit leaders should look for an opportunity to apply these lenses *every day* at work.

4.2 Distributing from the Center: Positional and Multidirectional

Related to the previous theme, future forms of leadership must focus on where people position themselves relative to others, with an ability to shift that location in multidirectional ways. In other words, to meet the inclusive and collaborative ideals described in the previous section, leaders should both think about where they locate themselves in their organizational spaces and do everything possible to connect with others at every institutional level. They are what could be called "positionally minded."

One participated summed it up this way:

> I used to see leadership very much as the head goose in a triangle at the head of the flock, and that has changed. For a visual metaphor, I think the leader is somebody at the center of the flock. I also think that the ball can be passed, that a really effective leader can hand off. What I mean by the ball is the main idea or the main intention, with some trust that it will be handed back to them.

Note how positioning oneself at the center differs from traditional, hierarchical notions of governance, while still providing room to lead. It also places a person in more direct and immediate relation to as many people within an organization as possible, reducing the distance between leaders and followers. This is also why I've chosen to use the back and forth arrows in the Figure 3 visualization of leadership standpoints. Leading from the center is only useful to the extent that it manifests a relationship between these qualities and practices with actual people. Good leadership cannot be based on unidirectional patterns.

Indeed, distributing from the center may mean upending previous theories of leadership completely. An interviewee told us they had:

leadership power as a young person at 25 years old and I really thought I needed to know the answers, have the answers and felt threatened if I didn't. "Threatened" might not be the word. The right word might actually be "exposed." [I] felt exposed if I didn't. And now I really work hard to build teams where I'm the dumbest person in the room. Making sure that we hire folks that have expertise in areas that I don't have expertise [in] so that we build a really round[ed], successful team where they can go and do the things again that are interesting and exciting to them. And so now when I don't know something, I'm okay with saying, "I don't know, somebody else hopefully knows that or we'll go and learn it together."

Letting down one's guard to engage in mutual learning remains central to this form of leadership. If you position yourself at the top of a triangle, then others have to position themselves in a subservient role. On the other hand, if the leader distributes from the center, it communicates that they are leading by working with others – and *need* others.

One participant underscored that, "Leading doesn't always mean that you're out front ... it means also encouraging the people with you to come along for the ride." One fellow praised their boss, since "What I really value about her leadership style is her ability to really be comfortable with just giving the autonomy out to her staff underneath her." Another leader was praised in similar terms:

I've learned from my direct supervisor at work, who really invests in or grants a lot of autonomy to staff and, in particular I think, has been really a strong believer in staff. Regardless of background or age or kind of educational status ... there's a very egalitarian approach to his leadership style, which is very much based on what people produce in their output at work and their skills as opposed to their credentials.

In these characterizations, leaders collaborate with staff and allow them freedoms that communicate trust and a belief in their work while maintaining high performance expectations.

This recognition about distributing from the center focuses an idea that one simply cannot go it alone in practicing leadership. Sometimes this means focusing strategically on particular people to get work done, while maintaining an inclusive orientation with all staff.[43] One participant said about another leader: "he's also very big with pushing this idea that in order to get things done, you need to find your agent of change ... your ally, whether it's on the board or in another department or whoever it is." At the heart of such leadership

---

[43] This theme accords with work on "leader-member exchange theory," which highlights how, over time and often unconsciously, leaders come to support some staff while excluding others in patterned ways (Lunenburg 2010).

is a repositioning of oneself in a central but reciprocal organizational role. Future nonprofit leaders should be attuned to the ins and outs of positionality, meaning that they are strategic about where they are operating from and what viewpoints those positions include and preclude. At the center of the flock, one is ready to lead but also break patterns where necessary to let others shine.

In this view, leadership should be multidirectional and dynamic. Even if inhabiting lower- or mid-level roles within an organization, many felt validated by learning that they can exert leadership skills wherever they go. One participant told us,

> You don't have to be the CEO or the executive director to be a leader. I think you can be impactful and effective in different ways. I think this idea of leadership isn't always that people follow you. I think that's changed ... it's more about bringing people with you. If you can get people on board and to all be working towards some goal together, then you've been effective as a leader.

This reorientation involves gaining a sense that one has more power than they may have thought, working with others toward a purpose, and sometimes placing responsibility on the group over and above individual efforts.

Distributing from the center invokes employees' agency and dignity. Discussing her boss's approach, an interviewee mentioned that "she trusts her staff to let them do their jobs ... And so I get the flexibility to develop things that are interesting to me ... and make mistakes or get it right based on ... learning and trial and error." The fellow told us their boss provided useful support when that's needed, while signaling to others that their own contributions are inherently valued. The verb "distributing" was chosen to represent the many practices that leaders will engage in, such as informing, delegating, and conversing with relationality and reciprocity.

Distributing from the center is a commitment to continuous learning (combining with another leadership standpoints theme). Instead of viewing leaders as always having the answers, those using this perspective find ways to prompt others toward diagnoses and solutions. One participant mentioned how, with a boss she often looked up to, "I would go and say, 'Here's the thing I'm really struggling with.' And so really instead of doing that 'she's come and asked for help therefore I've been knighted into solving her problem,' [she's] really helping me come to my own solutions. I always appreciate that in a leader." Those answers may not be known to either the leader or the direct report, but with enough trust-filled distribution of responsibility, there's an expectation that solutions can be found.

Distributing from the center further connects with the diversity theme. The metaphor of being at the center of the flock is an anti-hierarchical strategy. Yet *who* is doing the distributing should focus nonprofits' structural features. One fellow related her own nonprofits' disconnects on this matter:

> In my own organization, where the higher up in the hierarchy you get, the whiter it gets, despite the fact that 90% of our clientele are people of color, despite the fact that 90% of our staffers – not quite 90 but it's pretty close – 90% of our direct staff are people of color yet most of our senior leaders are white. And what does that mean for the policies and procedures that we develop for staff? What does that mean for the policies and procedures that we develop and advocate for, for clients? . . . really digging into that as a theory of leadership would be something that would be greatly on my mind.

There are more questions raised than answers provided here, but to ignore these systemic features of many nonprofits highlights a need to speak to more stakeholders. By consciously working across the nonprofit in multiform ways, and making sure that others are included in decision-making, future leadership is put within more people's reach. This means being aware of one's and others' standpoints individually, organizationally, and relative to larger structural problems.

This pillar reinforced how leaders must apply thinking about culture and power to all aspects of their leadership. Power is seen as a means of combating actions that promote inequity. One fellow said: "a best practice is using the power that, the leaders using the power that's given to them based on the hierarchy, to actively dismantle that hierarchy or actively work against it." Of consequence, frequently our interviewees put the mundane rather than grand areas of organizational life at the center of such work:

> Since the fellowship, I've been thinking a lot just about this white dominant culture piece. And I think that despite always trying to make the best decisions, I've just been thinking a lot about decisions that I make because it's just ingrained to me, this white dominant culture. And I think in my current role, it's just even more prevalent. A lot of the staff . . . My supervisor is constantly talking to me about how they lack "professionalism." And lately since the fellowship, I've been thinking a lot about, is it that they lack professionalism, or are we projecting . . . white dominant culture?[44] And personally, lately I've been struggling with how do I combat that?

Such remarks were central to a lot of our interviewees' thinking. In a telling example, one participant elaborated further:

> At the nonprofit that I worked at, we were talking about, and I can't remember the details of it, but essentially we were talking about promotions and salary schedules and how to do reviews and . . . the reason why we were talking

---

[44] Gray (2019: para 1) argues that, indeed, "Professionalism has become coded language for white favoritism in workplace practices that more often than not privilege the values of white and Western employees and leave behind people of color."

about it [was] because there wasn't a formal written policy but basically the policy that was proposed was just a reiteration of just the status quo . . . which is really entrenched in a history of a power dynamic and white supremacy basically. I don't know if that was too much of a leap for you. But that's how I see a lot of organizational structure, is stemming out of slavery basically. And so I think the best leaders are the ones who were like, "Okay, why are we doing it this way?" Is it just because that's how everybody else does it and what are the consequences of doing it that way and is there maybe a better way that's in line with the values of the organization . . . being able to be critical and question and see places where things could be better, more equitable or fair or more just.

To act positionally and multidirectionally is to situate oneself in long-term, broad contexts rather than short-term, narrow circumstances. Leadership aligns the past, present, and future without getting sidetracked by or disconnecting these elements from the seemingly routine functions of everyday working life.

At the same time, the idea of distributing from the center can certainly be applied in leadership training itself (see Figure 4). One fellow mentioned that some colleagues in the program were in a "hierarchical" and "prescriptive environment" that provoked much thought among their group. Distributing from the center doesn't obviate that there may be times and places where a hierarchical style may be fitting, but it calls into question the continuing dominance of this approach for leadership in and across organizations. According to one person: "I think some

Figure 4 Leading from the center. Photo courtesy of the NYCTLF.

of those folks that were coming from larger, more hierarchical organizations; they felt very much like the decision makers and recognized that they were in a position of power and tried to be equitable, but that they still had the final say." Under these terms, it becomes incumbent on leaders to foster less triangular organizational forms.

Leadership development programs should explicitly articulate this perspective. One fellow shared that the training itself "emphasize[d] non-hierarchical leadership," inviting leaders who "valued input from their staff and from colleagues as well, instead of it just being purely directive." It wasn't just the training, but the modeling of this principle from staff, trainers, and mentors that had an effect on participants:

> I think you can have the idea of a leader as being on the top of a pyramid. But then there's other leaders who are maybe, I don't know what the metaphor would be, but supporting people from behind. And I always got this sense that the teachers and the presenters [in the NYCTLF] were all people who were very, very good and experts and obviously had a lot of experience and could . . . be the one who calls all the shots, or sitting at the top of the pyramid. [Yet] I always got the sense that they were really just supporting and pushing and empowering other people to do their best work instead of being the ones to take the credit for [it].

Whether the leader is at the center of the flock, leading from behind, or perhaps leading through some other fractal metaphor that moves beyond hierarchical relations, the principle remains the same: leading with participation and positionality in mind; being careful to not "go it alone" or, as one person put it, "put the ego aside and really connect with someone else and help guide them through whatever it is that they need."

One final aspect of distributing from the center is that leadership doesn't need one conclusive definition. There are different ways of leading, although fellows asserted that those different ways of leading should still remain supportive rather than dominating with others. One interviewee said,

> I used to think that a leader was someone who really captured the space and was really dynamic. And, I think that is one style of leadership, and it can be a very effective one. But I think I see more too, now, that there is a lot of room for different styles of leaders, and that there can be a type of leadership where you're not necessarily the star of the show, but you still have a lot of confidence and authority in your opinions, and also take a lot of input from other people to help form those opinions.

In this characterization, charisma is a sufficient but unnecessary condition for leadership. So long as one has put their people and organization first, operating in positional and multidirectional ways, there's a variety of styles that may fit.

4.3 Leading from the Heart: Socially and Ecologically Compassionate

The interviews revealed an overriding concern for leadership that's both socially and emotionally intelligent and concerned with whole people and organizations. In this sense, the opposite of leading from the heart is leadership that's chronically logical or rational, with little care for people, nor attentive to the social world and cultures developing within the institution. One participant summed this up as "socially compassionate," while another stated, "I was just shocked by how compassionate the program was."

We heard repeatedly that leaders should be willing to speak to and learn from holistic, multifaceted people and organizations. As a key feature of leadership standpoints, seeing people partially as only one label or another, or failing to see an organization as an emerging ecology with many moving parts, would translate to leading with a selective sense of the individuals' present and the systemic nature of organizational challenges.

Fellows saw this theme as a distinctive feature of their leadership training itself. One related: "I saw the value of our common thread of empathy that ran through pretty much every presentation." The program's administrators were described in terms of having "a very warm and personable approach to leadership. I think that kind of human centered personal leadership really came from them and their personality types and what they value as leaders, which is great." Similarly, a fellow remarked that "I feel like a lot of the staff were very empathetic, both in the way that they taught, because I experienced them as teachers, but also in the content that seemed to be driving the way that they presented ideas of leadership. Empathy was a common thread." I can testify to observing this firsthand: one noteworthy feature of every session is how the program's director always arrived early and stood at the front door to greet and have a conversation with each participant as they entered, setting a welcoming tone. From the program's beginning, another fellow mentioned how "the first thing that I felt was that we were there to be nurtured and making our own rules when we came in for how we would proceed and what was important to us, what our values were." The fellows felt an empathy directed toward them that expressed a belief in their growth and agency.[45]

In characterizations drawn from when constructing this theme, the fellowship was described as "intentional and very person centered, heart centered, love centered. There's a lot of leading from the heart happening." This way of approaching others may come natural to many people, but if there's any lesson here, it's that this is a skill set that must be added to one's leadership repertoire –

---

[45] Empathy is a cornerstone of "emotional intelligence" theory (Goleman 2006).

as an approach that demonstrates to others that they matter – an expansion of standpoints. The terms that arose in this theme included "considerate," "supportive," "kind," and having "gratitude" and "appreciation," in particular. Research has found that leaders "can positively influence perceived performance by creating work groups wherein members feel valued and appreciated, which then fosters an emotional attachment and commitment ... [with] the ability to directly influence perceived nonprofit performance by being more transformational" (Brimhall 2019: 44).

Critically, this type of leadership emphasizes assets rather than deficits. As defined by one fellow: "the fellowship, I think, really took a very human oriented perspective towards leadership. I remember that there was a lot of certain things around personality testing and how to bring out the best in yourself and in employees, based on their strengths rather than their weaknesses." Exhibiting socially compassionate leadership means finding what's good, works, and can be built on in helping others develop to their maximum potential.

The second part of leading from the heart moves beyond caring for people, however. It involves a recognition of people and organizations as holistic and being an advocate for the multiform nature of individual and collective systems. According to one fellow:

> I felt like there was a lot of holistic awareness of the whole person that came through in all of the leadership teaching, where it wasn't just about a model, but it also considered the different experiences of everyone in the room and an awareness of everyone in the room ... that was an approach that was very functional, for me, as someone practicing.

Partly, this approach acknowledges that there's always more to know about people and organizations than whatever one currently thinks. Ineffective leaders come to premature, closed conclusions about people and groups that forgo future learning and the capacity for change. All this begs a dynamic rather than static view of others that create spaces where everyone counts.

Leaders have to reach as many parts of an organization as possible to perform ecological compassion. One interviewee mentioned how, "I've worked at five different agencies and seen five different CEOs, and some embody the ideals of leadership more than others or are more effective, I should say, in reaching the whole organization as a leader ... I think not everyone who has the position of authority always translates into being a leader."[46]

Similar to the distributing from the center theme, having a less hierarchical organizational setup isn't just a matter of creating equitable and inclusive

---

[46] This distinction between being in a position of authority and actually exercising leadership skills is also made in Heifetz, Grashow, and Linsky (2009).

climates but of making a leader's ability to reach many parts of an organization more likely. For one person, "At the core I always have felt that leaders should be champions for everybody ... and always working on what's good for the group." In sum, "I really think the best leadership practices out there are just the ones that challenge you as a manager to know your people ... how you have to continuously make genuine connections with people in order to manage them." These scenarios can only come to life when thinking about an organization and its people with a localized lens.

What's the effect of operating in this way? One term that arose was "healing." Leaders with this level of responsiveness and engagement with others, at all levels of the organization, promoted an almost spiritual level of reflection and commitment about mission-focused work. One interviewee found an instructor's session distinctive in this regard: "It felt like a closing out and healing session and he facilitated, through a couple of books ... one of them is called *The Circle Way* ... and felt like something that I wanted to bring to my organization." For future nonprofit leadership, the metaphor of the circle could actually serve as a defining quality: staff expect rounded leaders, who in turn see themselves within a circle of influence in which everyone contributes and supports one another.

5 The Secondary Dimension: Performance

The secondary dimension of leadership standpoints centers various aspects of nonprofit leadership performance. Where the previous dimension focused on building an inclusive ecology at every turn, here nonprofit leaders' actions seek to build climates where outputs, deliverables, or visions can be met. In this section, we'll cover four means shared for putting these ideals into practice.

5.1 Stretching toward a Higher Place: Brave and Visionary

A theory of leadership for future nonprofit professionals should incorporate the idea of helping everyone reach new heights. Future leaders will need to provoke aspirational work that rises above the status quo. To do so demands courage and vision, characteristics that surfaced repeatedly across our interviews. One participant shared that model nonprofit leaders are "Intellectually curious, brave. Brave should probably be at the top of the list because the people that I came into contact with are doing such challenging work," and "in the room as we were taking the fellowship, they were seeking to improve themselves constantly," or "self-improving." Another noted that leaders must be "deeply committed to the cause." Great leaders were described as having "their eyes on the future and not just in a where-they're-going-in-their-career perspective, but thinking about their institution and thinking about the state of the field in general." Alternating between local and global perspectives, nonprofit leaders look outside themselves for inspiration and motivation.

Other terms that arose included "change maker, outspoken, mission driven ... not a rebel, but somebody who has the courage to just break from the status quo," and "effective, well-managed, [and] daring." This captures the relationship between brave and visionary qualities: you have to be willing to stretch and even make unpopular decisions but do so with the best interests of people and communities in mind. These ideas served as a lasting inspiration for fellows themselves, one of whom shared:

> Leading is what I need to learn more of. I think leading is about setting a course with vision and using all different sorts of means to have people follow along. That can sometimes mean letting them lead so you're not necessarily at the head of the pack ... setting vision and keeping direction is how I could summarize it.

Here, the community and diversity themes join with values and goals that drive on-the-ground actions.

Specific people in our interviewees' lives provided stimuli for this theme. One person shared about the determination that she observed in an admired leader:

> I think that as a woman of color, she had encountered, I think she had to overcome a lot of prejudice or bias, to be in a position of leadership, I think that she had to overcome a lot ... I found her to be very level-headed too and really able to let everything just roll off her back.

The comparison between the interviewee's own mistakes and the steady visioning of this leader spoke volumes:

> I wasn't as effective in my role because I was bumming out over people not liking me and [the] sense that I got from her was, it just seemed like it never even was something that would register for her. She was able to focus, she cared about the important things and she didn't let the other things affect her.

This bravery was also seen as vital in creating a strong work culture. Having a thick skin is central to such leadership or, as one fellow put it, to "have a growth mindset and being able to persevere when things are tough within the organization or certain projects just get really, really complicated."

To stretch toward a higher place implicates a future and movement focus. Note the following interviewee's emphases on "moving forward" and similar terms stressing how much leaders can elevate their organization and staff:

> I really, really respected and still respect and value my supervisor there who is the director of education policy ... The reason why I think of her as a great

leader [is] that she's able to balance moving forward organizational goals, moving forward programmatic goals for the education program, and also providing professional development opportunities for her staff and making sure that her staff tapped into those larger goals of the organization and the program, so that no one feels as though they're just doing this task because they're told to do it. They really see how it fits into the larger work ... I trusted the decisions that she was making because ... she made the time to explain how she was making those decisions, right? So that we could learn what goes into creating strategies and moving work forward.

In essence, fostering an infectious feeling of momentum, accomplishment, and building others' capacities must be a part of this visioning.[47] One fellow told us about their boss in this regard: "she really just saw potential in me and worked with me to build it, and really helped me find my voice as a leader. And then she promoted me pretty quickly to manage a small team, and I think without that opportunity, I wouldn't be here."

Using language filled with movement constitutes one way to put these leadership goals into practice: forwarding, advancing, processing, and more to build mission-focused buy-in. Providing staff and stakeholders with a clear sense that you have the courage to take on difficult tasks, to persevere through challenges, and to fulfill visions all contribute to this picture. Celebrating minor milestones is also important in working toward grander visions. One fellow said:

> [it's the] essence of bravery, being able to speak up when either something's not working well or something could be working better. Being able to celebrate the small wins ... nonprofits are always under [pressures]: not enough money, not enough time, not enough people to do anything and so it can feel you're never making progress and the missions are often taking on big problems, so it can feel like you're not making any progress ... [so] find victories and focus on positive movement forward, rather than dwelling on the enormity of social injustice or whatever it is that they're taking on.

Making some progress, any progress, can be an accomplishment, but taking long-term visions and reducing them to shorter-term, everyday goals provides the needed motivation to keep going in organizations working on society's most pressing challenges.

Although bravery plays a role in leadership excellence, a major part of being visionary is getting people to stretch beyond their current abilities. We heard from one fellow that the best parts of leadership training involve "pulling things out of people and getting them to stretch a little bit, particularly people who are

---

[47] Lencioni's (2006) work underscores the differences between stellar teams that are results focused, make themselves accountable, commit to clear collective objectives, surface conflict, and create safe, trustful spaces to have a voice, with dysfunctional teams manifesting poor performance, high turnover, repetition, little honesty about problems, and a fear of speaking up.

not comfortable speaking." This supportive coaching role means, as one fellow mentioned about an observed leadership approach, "seeing how you could push someone in a way to help them either challenge what it is that they're thinking or get to the next plane."

Nonprofit leadership training made some fellows realize how they were not being brave enough in their work. After a session on developing effective meeting practices, one person shared how: "I started to realize a lot that those were the meetings I was having, where I was often the passive person." Leadership programs can provide what Palfrey (2018) calls both the safe and the brave spaces that participants need to develop or, as one fellow shared, "providing an environment where it's safe to make mistakes ... It's just an opportunity to learn from that."

Helping people grow in ways that they had not thought possible is connected to a belief that everyone can stretch toward a higher place. One fellow remarked about a favorite leader: "I've watched her career evolve. She really has a capacity to coach people up. She said she's able to see the potential of people from any background and any experience, and bring them up and elevate them through these cultural institutions." Brave and visionary leaders work hard to see the latent abilities within each person.

Leaders should themselves stretch toward integrity. One fellow was inspired by Barack and Michelle Obama. She mentioned that Barack's consensus-building work was the first time she had seen that approach in action at such a high level, along with Michelle's campaign slogan that when "'they go low, we go high,' that really resonates with me. I think leaders have a responsibility to work with the highest ethical standards possible, and I think very frequently people don't do that. And those are two examples of people that I think really lived their values and I admire that." To do leadership well, one must stake out the high-level ethical values that they will live, modeling integrity for others.

Being visionary comes with some qualifications, however. One interviewee clarified how leadership visioning relates to the previously mentioned distributing from the center theme:

> If you take your vision for, let's say, a museum, and drive it all yourself as the leader, if you're a single leader, it is going to lack some of the power that it could otherwise have. So, you read in the books about inspiring people to see your vision or follow your vision, but you don't read about, or at least I haven't, how you can compel people to take it on for themselves, to own it ... We do mission moments here ... At the beginning of every all-staff meeting, we invite a given staff member to come up and talk about ... the outward-facing aspect of the museum, how it impacts audiences is how I think about it. That's a pretty

good example of that because for somebody to devise that, even though it's just five minutes, and then present it, puts them in the mindset of how do I own this, how do I personalize this, how do I internalize this?

How a vision is administered should be at the core of every nonprofit leader's thought processes. Similarly, one participant noted that "there's the school of thought that says that the leader has the vision, the people follow the vision, and that's just a formal structure that you adhere to. I think it's more complicated than that, and I like the idea that the vision is informed by everyone and driven by the leader." One fellow said they considered themselves a good leader, but where they struggle more is in management, particularly in laying out and executing certain tasks. Being visionary involves the skills of follow-through and implementation, so collaborative leadership and management must be mutually implicated.

5.2 Inspiring Confidence: Intentional and Responsive

Aside from exhibiting bravery and supplying visions that can help everyone stretch in their abilities, leaders were also described as inspiring confidence through their intentionality and responsiveness. Where intentionality describes the deliberate, detailed, and practical focus of nonprofit leaders, responsiveness gets at the sense of a two-way immediacy that our interviewees found important. These highlight how vision requires implementation.

Leaders make themselves accessible and inspire confidence in their staff. As noted about the NYCTLF program itself, "being intentional I think came up a lot," with leaders valuing "the diversity and inclusion of their organization and the people within the organization." Finding ways to connect to each individual is part of leadership or "being mindful of the person that is the individual that we're leading" and responsive to their needs and interests. As one person said, a nonprofit leader is "someone who is available to their staff."

For some fellows, these were hard-won lessons. One person noted:

> I've also learned from different bosses that I've had over the course of my career, what styles of leadership I don't think are as effective. I've learned from my own experience, I think, being frustrated sometimes by leaders at an organization who haven't been as hands on, that I really value not being micromanaged, but a boss that's willing to roll up their sleeves and contribute to the work.

Where micromanagement may certainly offer one unwelcome extreme, a general expectation is that leaders are engaged in and have a clear sense of everyday organizational activities.

To inspire confidence, leaders might best be characterized as adaptive actors. The Hersey–Blanchard situational leadership model was sometimes referred to as a memorable framework. A distinctive feature of the model involves the shifts that leaders need to make between providing direction, being supportive, delegating work to others, and engaging in intentional one-on-one coaching.[48] The model calls for leaders to be deliberate and flexible with people, never fully sticking to one style over others.

Being deliberate further means making a conscious effort to surface habits and behaviors that affect the organization and those it serves. Good leaders do all that is possible to avoid being on autopilot. One participant shared: "leadership is, or should at least try to be, intentional, with a real thoughtful understanding of how your actions as a leader impact everyone around you." Being intentional is never just an individual enterprise, however, since it develops via one's responsiveness to others and ethical considerations. For example, these could involve "deeper conversations about the nonprofit management, nonprofit strategy, intentionality in how, as a leader, you manage your group dynamics. The ideas of intentionality, regarding mission and mission drift and when to say no to money."

Nonprofit leaders also apply the same type of purposeful intentionality to their own career development. They have short- and long-terms goals, engaging in the challenge of continued growth. One interviewee said that "you can see their potential as they move, as they build their career." One participant shared how they had:

> been ascending as a leader in my organization at that time [when they came to the fellowship], but I had really been learning things on the fly. I think for me it was really helpful just to have the opportunity to step back and reflect about what kind of leader I wanted to be and how I could really think more strategically about leadership and management.

Nonprofit leaders simply cannot be on the go and doing all the time; they must carve out space to chart their own, intentional directions, which serves as a model for others.

Being practical and conscientious inspires confidence among nonprofit stakeholders. Leaders are "driven without being aggressive, and detail-focused," both down-to-earth and aspiring toward higher purposes. One interviewee mentioned:

> I'm now in a state where, the practice is really important. Meaning, I'm in this place of . . . okay, it worked in the lab, but how do you make it work in the situation that you're in? How do you make it work in the context that we're all living in? How do you handle the specific, really difficult, societal, structural problems that we all face? . . . And with any group of people?

---

[48] See, for example, the four-part image at Kuhn (2016).

As much as nonprofit leaders may be driven by useful theories, they put themselves in experimental positions where they're forced to practice what they preach. Since the stories that people tell often conflict with the stories that they live,[49] theories have to be made interactive and situational, with room for responsiveness and potential redirection.

Intentionality and responsiveness are most differentiated from working in prefigured ways. A fellow told us that, prior to the leadership training program:

> I was coming from a pretty reactionary place in my leadership ... [but] I read a little bit about adaptive leadership and it really spoke to me. But I felt like reading by myself only took me so far. And being in a room with other individuals, in the nonprofit sphere, it escalated how quickly, it amplified how quickly I could learn. You learn fast. I learned more.

This fellow put leadership development between theory and practice, making living, breathing human beings a core part of the experience, with a realization that "you also as an organization need to be responsive to the community and that involves listening to what the community has to say," again emphasizing the multidirectional nature of leadership.

In these terms, we heard about someone who "is an undercover phenomenal leader, I say, because in staff meetings ... she wouldn't usually boast herself. But one-to-one, she was so intentional with her management. So I think she was a great person in my life." This intentionality and responsiveness must be connected to the ongoing cycle of planning, implementing, evaluating, and improving through which leaders orchestrate results. For instance, a leader might build a diverse coalition of staff within a nonprofit to plan the annual budget, delegate responsibilities for implementation, and then orchestrate weekly one-on-one meetings to determine if changes need to be made in allocations along the way. With a connection to the following leadership standpoints theme, such intentionality and responsiveness can build climates of continuous learning.

All this means that leadership development should awaken or further latent abilities in oneself and others. One interviewee underscored how:

> going through that program, I felt like I was waking up a little bit ... I'd had two kids and I'd been working and ... I hadn't thought about leadership for myself in quite some time. And so doing that [NYCTLF] program really, it woke me up and made me access parts of myself that I hadn't been getting to for a while.

Leadership development programs can inspire confidence and sensitize participants to these themes.

---

[49] The stories told versus stories lived distinction can be found in Pearce (2009: 212).

5.3 Creating an Appetite and Opportunities for Continuous Learning: Curious, Generative, and Teachable

Similar to the previous theme, leaders are deliberate and interactive but also genuinely inquiring, creative, and humble in the service of unmitigated learning. No organization can advance without continuous learning, but that space has to be consciously constructed. One fellow said what made one leader "a really great person to work with and work for is her approach to everything is with lots of reflection and thoughtful questioning . . . I feel like she's an ongoing learner forever and that she approaches most things where we're going to learn together." Given the demands of nonprofit life, this may be the skill set most easily lost or the most difficult to keep salient. One person said the people they most admire as leaders simply "promote ideas."

Continuous learning maintains a sense of the who, what, when, and where. One fellow spoke at length about this need, among other priorities that leaders face:

> We tend to focus on the fiduciary, budgets, or strategic [planning], where we're heading and how we're going to get there. But that generative space, that's an idea that I think is really important. The idea that you create as a leader time and space for people to have new ideas. I don't think you have an engine on your car unless new ideas are coming in, and you have to make some space and time for that, which has changed my perception of how I want to work, or how I would want my team or organization to work . . . Generative work, you need time to settle and let your mind wander . . . I've also been working a lot with my organization's work culture and how to impact that directly. I've been doing these roundtable sessions for the staff, which are not formal all-staff meetings, and they're not mandatory. There's no leader. So, they're a voluntary roundtable on a particular topic. They've been really great for morale, but also for idea generation and for making people feel heard.

There's a lot to unpack in this passage but, at its core, is a commitment to opening space for others to impact goals: a passion for diversity and inclusion, for getting more in control of the organization's attentional flows, for distributing from the center, and more. In particular, this form of leadership is highly invitational and doesn't pretend to know the best courses of action without open input from others. The generation of ideas can't happen without a curious orientation that provides room for multiple stakeholders (see Figure 5).

At the heart of continuous learning is self-awareness, an attention to self that's unsettled and always in pursuit of further knowledge and effective practice. One fellow said this means "really being mindful about giving myself time to reflect on my leadership style and thinking about ways that I can improve, seeing what's out there, having a community." To grow, there has to

Figure 5 Learning for performance. Photo courtesy of the NYCTLF.

be "creative friction." Any tools that can help one get a greater view of their tendencies can help toward these goals. One participant explained:

> The pieces of leadership that I always really enjoyed are any sort of assessment that gives you a self-reflection … and then you can turnkey it to know your staff. So things like the Myers–Briggs[50] or … I'm forgetting, there's this other one, but there's those personality tests you can take and then you know what triggers you, what motivates you. I found that I've been sharing that with the people that I've managed, and I think it's really helpful for them to understand how I operate naturally, and then for me to understand how they operate. I am very open with them that if I'm being too much this way, professionally, you could tell me that you need me to be more this way.

Repeatedly, we heard comments such as, "I think leadership starts with a full understanding of self, so whatever practice it is, I think it has to start with a very intensive self-reflection." One fellow even urged the fellowship to use more of a diagnostic approach throughout.

One caveat provided by the NYCTLF and similar programs bears mentioning. People often think they can be the judge of themselves, which would be naïve under the terms of leadership standpoints. To gain accurate self-perceptions, one

---

[50] Although the fellow's comments rightly concern the need for self-assessments that can guide leadership training, the Myers–Briggs inventory has received copious criticism for its flaws. See, for example, Stromberg and Caswell (2015). Flexible and situational assessments such as DiSC® are better suited to the characteristics of leadership standpoints.

must seek insights from others; a person cannot accurately perceive themselves via self-reflection alone. This is where peer coaching and networking can play an important role. Even some conversations with people who are trusted and admired can help build this competency, for instance, by asking questions such as: What have you experienced as my greatest strength? I observe you are good at X; how did you learn that? How might I do that? A participant brought this idea to an institutional level: "I remember one colleague, for example, had been talking about bringing in someone to really do an audit of their organizational structure, and that was really useful, I think, for me, in terms of catalyzing some thinking about where my organization could improve." Useful peer coaching and assessment can range from formal features of leadership development programs to informal conversations over coffee.

As another consideration, excellent nonprofit leaders continually look back to look forward. They remain unsettled and teachable, never completely satisfied with the current state of play in their fields, yet open to the possibility for course corrections given new information. One fellow told us how "I learned a lot of my work in the field, through trial and error and by going into situations in public schools in Queens and having to tango with the circumstances that young people are facing in schools, in Queens. So, a lot of the learning that I experienced is by practice, is by failure in the field." The fellows emphasized that negative forms of learning should play a role in leadership development: not just learning by doing what's right but making slipups and thinking through steps forward. Here's how one person put it:

> Learning from negative examples, I think, is something that hasn't been stressed that much, at least in the exposure that I've had to leadership and leadership practice discussions. I feel like I have learned so much from the people that I feel are doing things that I would want to do differently. That's shaped me, I think as much if not more than people who've been supportive or the model leaders . . . in my experience it's been actually more helpful to learn from the negative examples.

The imprint left on one's memory from bad experiences and practices should inform a theory of leadership as much as optimal constructions. Just as many business schools have classes in subjects such as "company failures," one implication is that leadership training programs could spend an entire session or more on "terrible leadership."

Many of the fellows' comments connected continuous learning to the skill of admitting weaknesses, signaling leaders' humility and vulnerability. One person said:

> I've really appreciated when leaders have been open to feedback and input, and also criticism. I've been trying to emulate that and take that even further with my staff, and try to give them a lot of input into the decisions that we make and empower them to have the information and access that they need to become leaders in their own right.

Another shared:

> I also really tend to bristle when organizations or leaders of organizations haven't been willing to acknowledge where they've made a misstep . . . where just being more concerned about being right or an image of oneself [becomes more important] than listening to feedback and being able to grow and change as more information comes out, or as the landscape changes.

Through an array of related phrasings, we heard that leaders should be open and honest, "acknowledge disruption," "not give people false confidence," and have "transparency about struggle or things not working," along with an "ability to be reflective and humble about their experience and still be learning and not this, 'I've had this X number of years career and therefore I already know all of this,' but really learning with us." About one respected leader, a fellow mentioned, "the humility and openness in which he taught us was again something to be mimicked and recreated." All of these terms relate to the conscientious crafting of trust and an accountability to others to which powerful figures hold themselves.

5.4 Taking Care of Oneself: Fueled and Well

Our interviewees highlighted how great nonprofit leadership must prioritize taking care of oneself. It's no use giving all of one's time and energies to other people and causes without taking the time to support one's self and health. In leadership, there's every reason in the world to put this need on the backburner for the sake of creating and implementing a vision and putting out the fires that will inevitably surface while making progress on difficult issues. Yet without the time and space to fuel oneself, a loss of the integrity that comes with rest and reflection can easily ensue, as can the burnout that creates exhaustion, bitterness, and anxiety for individuals and groups, among a host of well-documented, harmful effects (Maslach & Leiter 2008: para. 10). Our participants highlighted this surprising aspect of the fellowship itself, in learning to provide "time for yourself as a leader, and I think that's really important, because you can really wear yourself down." Some ways to de-stress include exercise, meditation, or anything else that can "re-energize" a person.

"Self-care" or "self-compassion" summarizes this perspective – and these acts are anything but fluffy or passive.[51] Overlapping with the socially and

---

[51] The work of Dr. Kristin Neff is especially compelling in this area. See her website: www.self-compassion.org.

ecologically compassionate theme, whole people need at least some attention to their own needs and what fuels the self: healthy food, time for family or friends, even reflective distance. One fellow cited this idea: "You need to have also opportunities to balance out where you're taking care of yourself and then you're able to take care of others." This is a standpoint that future generations of nonprofit leaders will need to step into.

The question of "wellness" in nonprofits loomed large for our interviewees. Since there's so much potential for diversity in leadership, and with so many being in leadership roles for the first time, our participants thought that the need to address self-supports is especially pronounced in the current climate. Without the lens of community and diversity, this insight would likely not be possible. Building an inclusive culture means caring about everyone's state of being. This is why the methods of "checking in" and "checking out" during each working day with staff have been supported in the organizational development literature (Kegan & Lahey 2016: 28–29, 102–103, 107, 148–149).

Organizations dealing with serious and, at times, highly discouraging public problems form formidable barriers to taking care of oneself. In particular, justice-based organizations where there's an attachment to the driving gravity of the work may prevent time for enjoyment or the lighter side of life. One fellow told us:

> we ignore [the] social-emotional competencies of adults, and we train every-one and we work with everyone on the assumption that everyone is at 100 percent all the time, emotionally competent and sound, which it just isn't the reality for anybody ... I think that there's a lot of work to be done around mental health and just care for employees and care for yourself as a leader, and looking into your own mental health.

Perhaps due to the type of discourse around performance that's so embedded in organizations, the expectation that everyone is operating at full capacity can easily push aside considerations of wellness and the ebbs and flows of one's attentions, feelings, and mindsets. This may also be why recent work in this area suggests that energy management is more important than time management (Schwartz & McCarthy 2017).[52] Leadership standpoints shift a view of performance to this more holistic and realistic view of human development.

Being well also means learning to lead from the standpoint of one's strengths. Along with the other themes already described, taking care of oneself means supporting that which is already working. One fellow told us that in joining the fellowship she realized that:

---

[52] Carving out space for this kind of leadership is also highlighted in the work of Marturano (2014), who advises using mindfulness every day, particularly through "purposeful pauses."

> what a lot of folks were looking for is how to develop leadership skills that are specific to you and . . . your organizational culture. But not waiting for the title that will give you the authority to be leader, if that makes any sense. That there's lots of different ways to have influence in leadership without thinking you need to be the E[xecutive] D[irector] on day one.

Being self-supportive means exercising leadership skills in a way that doesn't necessarily have to look the same for everyone and simply learning to do the best one can from a number of positions.

6 The Tertiary Dimension: Range

The tertiary dimension covers nonprofit leadership range. Where the previous dimension advances a climate of holistic performance, here attention is placed on the cross-disciplinary, networked, and stylistic range of nonprofit leaders. As the world's problems grow increasingly complex and "wickeder," generalists will have an advantage over specialists (Epstein 2019).[53] This isn't to diminish the importance of specialization but rather highlights how the next generation of nonprofit leaders will need an expansive toolkit from which to draw, to keep learning from others, and to cross domains of experience. In this section, I cover four means our interviewees shared for putting these ideals into practice.

6.1 Communicating through Effective Processes: Energetic and Eclectic

The importance of communication to leadership development came up frequently throughout the interviews. Two qualities emerged the most: bringing energy to leadership communication and having a range of eclectic methods for the different types of communication professionals will undertake. The fellows shared that they valued process-based leaders who can listen well and present effectively to multiple stakeholders, in particular. Being effective in these areas requires an ability to imagine and address others' standpoints.

Our participants viewed different charismatic styles as a way to advance the causes that nonprofits care about, meet different people where they're at, and align organizational passions with a performance of those commitments. One fellow highlighted the importance of "giving presentations that are really high energy but also have almost an economy of language. So you're being brief but also really targeted and specific and . . . the visuals support that as a way of just communicating effectively." One person said that they looked up to one leader in the following terms: "I think with his leadership style, I think he's able to

---

[53] Holt's (2019) review of the Epstein book fleshes out some core features relative to other popular work previously arguing that extreme specialization is most needed for achievement.

connect with his staff through his passion for the work. He's super, super passionate . . . People really gravitate towards that." The interviewees believed that public speaking to groups of all sizes would be a regular part of leadership, so it's critical to take the time to improve one's range in this and similar areas.

Some of the adjectives used to describe these skills involved both force and levity. Describing the qualities of peer leaders, one participant shared how they appreciated another person who is a "remarkably capable and charismatic speaker . . . you see the incredible strength and power and potential and capacity of him," while another "was great to work with and seems like someone who brightens up any group of which she's a part, and that's a great way to be a leader, just by being fun to be around." Such qualities go a long way toward establishing a leader as "someone you would follow into battle." Energy and a range of emotional and behavioral choices build admiration and followership.

The fellows further valued the importance of communication in meetings, especially for nonprofit leadership, using a range of processes to accomplish group goals. According to a participant:

> Some of the things that I remember that I then applied afterwards were more efficient meeting strategies. I remember we dedicated a good amount of time to different meeting types first of all . . . the number of people in the meeting, how the style of meeting would work better for different numbers of people, but also what the goal of the meeting was and how to – instead of just everyone's sitting in a room, sometimes there's an agenda – how you can make it more innovative and a space for idea sharing and creativity. I learned better communication practices more generally.

Although not necessarily on fellows' agendas coming into the fellowship, these communication forms were connected to productive and equitable organizational cultures. A fellow shared how:

> I was especially moved by and continue to use alternative meeting formats that we were taught there, ways to express individuality and work experience, and finally, work culture . . . just this idea of culture as something we are constantly swimming in that everybody is creating together has had a profound effect on how I do my work.

According to the interviewees, the next generation of nonprofit leaders should have a mix of facilitation tools to help people engage with others at a higher level.

Once again, the fellows linked this theme with diversity, community building, and distributing from the center through a noteworthy emphasis on nonprofit leaders' skills in communicating in many directions. A fellow articulated how a leader is "someone who is able to articulate their vision very well in a way that seems grounded . . . It's a really great communication skill, being able to communicate to different audiences and someone who doesn't lose sight of the inner workings of the organization, either." As one fellow put it, the importance of diverse "social skills, people skills" should not be underestimated by any aspiring leader. With relevance to other leadership standpoint themes, having the confidence to be self-critical is part of good communication skills: "I think leadership needs to involve a lot of listening. It needs to involve a willingness to be okay not knowing everything, and a willingness to own mistakes, and a willingness to own your decisions." Speaking with and assisting people at every organizational level is part of practicing eclectic communication skills. Culture cannot be separated from the quality of communication within an organization, so one way to start building a culture of conversation is to make it a strategic goal – linking the development of skillful, effective conversations to key organizational priorities (Credi & Ainsworth 2019).

6.2 Applying Polymathic Knowledge: Expert and Cross-Disciplinary

Nonprofit leaders should exhibit skillful, cross-disciplinary applications of knowledge. They have a breadth and depth of wisdom drawn from the many areas of working life and are typically some of the most polymathic figures in their organizations. Showing that expertise matters, one fellow described a memorable leader in these terms: "For her, she's [got] an extreme[ly] hard work ethic. Very knowledgeable on a lot of different topics. She's a go-to person. If I have any issues or things that I'm trying to wrap my head around, I run it by her and she gives really good advice." Moreover: "She has a lot of deep content expertise and is able to speak knowledgeably on, I think, most aspects of nonprofit leadership." In essence, when such leaders speak, they earn the respect of their peers and direct reports by exhibiting breadth.

Leaders were well regarded for their familiarity with wide information and the degree to which they allowed external data to inform their opinions. One person mentioned how "people's research and their background knowledge was profound and really impactful." Consistent with the other themes, it's not enough to simply have this knowledge – this expertise has to reflect collaboration. A fellow admired both the "depth in his expertise" and the humility and reflectiveness of one leader. Another remarked about how decision-making intentionally rooted in "evidence-based practices, and then moving forward in a way that you bring in people along with it" is essential.

Since leaders usually have broad information about an organization, collaboration and openness to other people and the environment become necessary to fill knowledge gaps. Aligned with the distributing from the center theme, a fellow described a colleague who became a chief operating officer and had:

> a really great approach to leadership where she's taking on a role where she doesn't necessarily have all the expertise in specific skill areas and really relies on her staff for that technical knowledge, but is still able to really be a strong leader in terms of determining the direction that the organization needs to go in and being able to see when people aren't delivering or performing in the way that they should be, and not hold[ing] back on that even if the person might be more of a technical expert.

This approach had an impact, as:

> I've grown as a leader in a space where I started as a technical expert. It feels intimidating to me, to think about taking on a leadership role where I'm not really . . . well-grounded in the details of the skills for the positions under me. And so, I really admire that mix of confidence and acknowledgment of where one's staff might be more knowledgeable than oneself in certain areas.

While seeking to learn as much as possible from all sources of knowledge, others' expertise is no threat in this form of leadership. The standpoints from which others can lead are seen as a gift rather than a liability to decision-making and influence. Again, this related to the idea that "you don't necessarily know best" and instead should "capture the expertise or the knowledge of the group." One interviewee reiterated their belief "in pulling expertise from lots of places to inform how you negotiate your organization's path forward." Great nonprofit leaders act from some standpoints in the overall network of others' standpoints, giving credit where credit is due and acknowledging their own limitations and need for others in amending or applying expertise.

Of note, all leaders need some expertise in financial matters. Although a leader should have a cross-disciplinary outlook, the fellows implied that this is an area for ongoing attention. One person pointed out how "the training that we had gotten on organizational finances was really helpful. I had been somewhat involved in the finances for our organization and definitely for my programs, but . . . I wasn't sure what was the way we did things versus [an] industry standard and norms." One fellow spoke about an NYCTLF instructor's workshop on "financial statements, and he broke down where this one nonprofit . . . where they went wrong. And I have sat through more than one class on financial statements and nonprofit financials and it is an achievement to make it interesting." Given the number of policies or regulations around financial matters and the impact of decisions about organizational budgets, numeracy skills – as they relate to larger fields of practice – must be a continuing concern for leadership development.

Additionally, the fellows viewed resource mobilization and its ties to financial concerns as a critical part of nonprofit leadership training. One fellow called for more training in fundraising. In practice, "there's all these things like crowdsourcing and fundraising ethics. There's just so much to cover, and it would be really important for any nonprofit professional to be ahead on." Fellows were looking for an integrated picture about monetary matters that was attentive to both one's present financial picture and how to best manage the organization's future numbers.

Overall, applying polymathic knowledge surfaced some factors that fellowships like the NYCTLF program could work on further. One participant said that the fellowship moving forward could do more "concrete skills based work. I think there were a lot of important discussions and opportunities for reflection" and "interpersonal dynamics," but even more applied work would help. Leadership development programs must concern themselves with application every step of the way. In the field of talent development, it's a long-standing truism that teaching isn't training (Biech 2017). The models many of us have inherited for how education works come from traditional classroom lecturing; but this is a limited framework for transferring learning from professional development programs to participants' working lives. Instead, training programs must conduct an analysis of the real needs that participants have and create curricula that get straight to the range of skills and applications that address these needs (Beebe, Mottet, & Roach 2012).

6.3 Seeking and Advancing Peer Support: Networked and Upwardly Mobile

A surprising finding from the interviews concerned the role of peers, mentors, and networks in leadership. Related to but distinct from the themes of distributing from the center and stretching toward a higher place, here participants underlined both the internal and the external presence of key actors in leaders' lives. When it comes to self- and other-mobility, the boundaries of organizations should be porous, reinforcing continuous learning through broad ranging networks. As a feature of leadership standpoints, leaders search for support and keep themselves current and connected (see Figure 6).

Operating from a range of standpoints, one fellow made clear to us that the term "networking" might as well be replaced with "informal peer support," which continues to constitute a good share of education in the nonprofit space:

> A lot of the learning I experience as peer is through peer friendships and peer communication, sharing resources. I do attend some conferences ... Honestly, the peer learning is more powerful than [any] particular conference

Figure 6 Networking. Photo courtesy of the NYCTLF.

> tends to be ... And I'm a part of an ... Aspiring Anti-racist Museum
> Educators Reading Group and that's actually where some of the most power-
> ful peer sharing and teaching and learning, in my experience, comes from.

Professional development cannot only be bound to workshops. There's wider support systems to tap into that many fellows naturally gravitated toward as they try to do their work in more informed and useful ways.

Our participants invoked the fellowship itself as a mechanism for modeling peer support and seeking upward career mobility. One person shared about a "colleague, another peer from the program ... [who] had used the fellowship as momentum for leveraging a promotion within his organization, and I think since then had gotten a couple. And so, that was inspiring too, just to see both people thinking about things in terms of their organization but also in terms of their own career trajectories." Consistent with the type of give and take observed in the other themes, seeing others go through leadership training and develop upward mobility provided an infectious momentum in others to seek out similar paths.

Having mentors outside of organizations or key personnel within them dedicated to networking and advancing emerging leadership can also help. Describing a mentor-matching initiative at work, one fellow described how:

> one thing that I'm really jazzed about right now in my organization is we have
> started a ... learning leaders program for our rising stars if you will. And for
> my organization, I'm a member of our senior management team and so each

of the people in our learning leaders program is paired with a mentor from a senior team.

Nonprofits must address the sustainability of talent in their organizations, thinking more strategically about the leadership pipeline.

One respondent found her role as a mentor to others particularly rewarding, highlighting how all leaders could do likewise. She shared that, for women of color especially, it's "that ability to network and to have someone in senior management who can help you navigate the politics or . . . early career mistakes that we all make." So it's critical to "provide leadership, mentorship, coaching for the next people who are going to replace us." Indeed, one way that leaders come to have applied, cross-disciplinary knowledge is through fellowship programs, building intentional networks, and by seeking out mentors and mentees.

One fellow related how:

> one of the special things about the Fellowship was the opportunity to share ideas between leaders of such different approaches and stripes and organizations and fields. That is really rare and really special, to cross-pollinate through different fields. I'm not sure there's many other examples of where that happens. I think that that might be really important for any leader going forward.

If a professional development training focuses solely on delivering content and excludes opportunities for peer learning, the experience will not be as impactful.

Being part of communities of practice around leadership development provides an opportunity to translate theory into collective actions. One participant raised the possibility of doing so through digital spaces. Given how everyone lives in both online and offline worlds now, they emphasized how this form of support would only help: "I would love to stay connected with that group through a forum or something like that where we can have that space, that digital space, and flexibility where we can put our thoughts and opinions and have those conversations that way." To make this work well, further thought could go into the architecture of digital supports for leadership development.

6.4 Anchoring Values with Idiosyncratic Styles: Stable and Lithe

For this final theme, we learned about an interesting paradox. Participants saw leadership as combining conscious, stable values and a steady hand with lithe, stylistic adaptations and room for idiosyncrasies. In a way, this final theme relates to the core emphases of the need for community and diversity that we heard about throughout the interviews and is representative of the findings for this project as a whole.

For leadership, it's important to have some uniting principles for practice, while leaving plenty of room for a diversity of styles, modes of behavior, ways of thinking, and context-sensitive adaptations that express the medley of humanity. That's leadership standpoints in a nutshell. It can be easy to get overly prescriptive about what leadership should or shouldn't be, so this theme reminds future leaders to search for useful guidance in this area while always leaving room for surprises or new learnings – other standpoints – to inform their thinking.

The fellows perceived stellar leaders as grounded. One person related: "I think everybody is looking for stability, and that's something very important a leader can provide even when they are not feeling it." Following the advice that "No matter what happens, act as if nothing has happened," the interviewee saw leaders as having a constancy in difficult situations, as people who can be reliably expected to maintain composure, even if others have difficulty doing so. We heard from another fellow, too, that "staying calm under pressure is a great leadership quality."

Many remarks highlighted this steadfast quality. Speaking about a boss one fellow looked up to, we learned how "She was managing a large team, but she seemed to really stay calm under pressure." One fellow positioned this expectation in numerical terms:

> She's also always at a five and a half. When she's flustered, sometimes it moves to a six, but that's rare. And so she's pretty unflappable in ways that are helpful when something really significant is happening ... The fact that she doesn't move very far from five and a half to 5.9, [that's] helpful and calming.

Leaders are expected to have an integrity, self-control, and poise from which they act – a foundational standpoint among their standpoints.

Yet being firm is only half of this equation. Flexibility is also at the core of leadership practices. An interviewee shared how important it is "to see yourself as a leader and how many different ways there are to lead." A fellow said that they valued leaders who "are willing to take a really firm stance on their ideals and ... also be willing to acknowledge when they have been wrong or could have done something better." One person told us about a boss who stood out, in this regard:

> In terms of leadership, she has a really direct and blunt style, but [is] also very supportive in her own way, and I've really enjoyed working with her. She just gets right down to business whenever we meet, to make the most of her limited time. And that's been really interesting, I think, for me too, especially as a woman, to see someone who takes less of a typically nurturing role but at the same time really wants to give back and support. It's been an interesting

model of leadership, to see someone who's very direct and no fluff or niceties, but at the same time is really supportive and wants the people she's working with to succeed.

Note the both/and quality of this characterization. The leader manifests a stable yet lithe paradox in her behavioral choices. She clearly has anchoring values but also adjusts her style in different situations. Too much firmness can be perceived as autocratic, while too much support may leave others directionless. It's similar to what Baxter and Montgomery (1996) call "relational dialectics," or the need to continually oscillate between two seemingly contradictory poles (e.g. independence and dependence) to establish a good relationship. Moreover, as Cameron et al. (2014: 59, 18, 83) highlight, great leadership is founded in competing values or "positive opposites" that "pursue several directions simultaneously," especially in attending to the underdevelopment of (or overemphasis on) creating, collaborating, controlling, and competing in an organization, while practicing the paradoxes of "autonomous engagement," "practical vision," "teachable confidence," and "caring confrontation." One fellow similarly observed in a leader how "she really adapts her style to the situation of what you need," showing that being stable – while being ready to be adaptable to others – underpins excellent nonprofit leadership.

This doubled expectation was brought to a head in observations about the fellowship environment. According to one participant:

> There was a wide range of types in my group. I think of some people as being dynamic and charismatic and being able to lead from a place of being inspiring. I also see others who are thinking more about laying solid foundations and creating a place that's structurally sound ... I also think that there are some people who are really passionate about this, serving a specific community and making sure that that community is given a platform for a voice.

Despite a range of styles one might exhibit, leadership is not a static, self-sealing enterprise. It is a "justified accommodation," where one holds firm to commitments but also allows room for change.[54]

A fellow mentioned how early diagnostics could help future leaders become more self-aware while navigating differences. Many of the fellows demonstrated their ongoing reflections about these matters. One person commented:

> There's this theory too that I love, and it's called your "ways of knowing." And it basically feels like everyone has a different way of knowing, and so that's how you should deliver feedback, based on a person's way of knowing. Some people are rule based and some people are social-emotional based. And

---

[54] For more on the idea of "justified ... accommodation," see Booth (2004: 52).

it's interesting, because I work with a lot of rule based people, whereas I am not that at all. I'm very driven by social connection. So my concern was always, will you like me? And their concern is more like, well, no one's right or wrong, what do you want me to do? And so I found that that's actually been really helpful for me, in knowing what type of knower you are.

Such a theory of leadership derives from a deep respect for one's own and others' proclivities but also centers on a moral concern for breaking beyond psychological and sociological boundaries to learn and grow.

Once again, our interviewees linked this theme with an overriding concern for inclusiveness and a broader picture of where leadership fits with the standpoints of racial and gender lenses, in particular. One fellow shared candidly that leadership training programs should not assume "we're all on a level playing field and that maybe some of us have different professional strengths and weaknesses, but that we're all sort of similarly minded and have had similar experiences, when that's just not the case." Instead, they should recognize "true diversity and the need for different leadership styles and how some fit better with [some] people than others and some are better fits for different organizations . . . like a menu of options instead of just one type of leader." If anything, these comments underscore how professional development training for leadership itself needs to do more to discuss idiosyncrasies, cultural differences, and the way that leadership can translate to varying styles and expectations across such disparate topics as finance and management. Starting from standpoints offers a platform for speaking about the different positionalities every person inhabits or how traditional approaches may be inadequate for capturing and prescribing leadership practices.

With relevance to this theme, terms such as "authenticity" have come under scrutiny in recent years. In popular culture, the idea of being firm or stable associates with what many perceive as authentic. As Alvesson and Einola (2019: 6, 9) argue, however, common allusions to authenticity tend to forward consistent and unitary senses of self (a "psychological reductionism") that belie the shifting, multiple, and socially situated selves that are always at play, as well as times when authenticity gets in the way of being helpful (they ask: what if a manager is an authentic jerk, after all?). Authentic notions of the self can further fail to consider power inequities. Parsing these distinctions, Jay and Grant (2017: 31–33) highlight the difference between a static notion of authenticity that presents people as fixed and wedded to past commitments at every turn and a "dynamic authenticity" that's grounded in values yet adaptive, future focused, and willing to change.

As one fellow said, a leader is "someone who is consistent and takes into account the history of the organization and the successes and failures that its had . . . can create a plan from that . . . [yet] is very flexible and creative in their thinking and can deal with change as it comes." It's about both stability and giving oneself and others the permission to play with possibilities, pursuing new selves and standpoints.

In the following final section, this Element's conclusions are brought to a head. I argue that nonprofit professionals should hew closely to leadership standpoints, in whole or part. As a guiding frame, it offers an approach that not only can be put into practice but addresses what stakeholders most want and need from nonprofit leaders.

7 Conclusion: Toward Leadership Standpoints for Nonprofit Practice

> If there's a way to distill those [leadership] takeaways and teach them, so you don't have to go through years of having good or bad bosses to get there, that'd be great.
> New York Community Trust Leadership Fellows alumnus

At the outset of this project, I told the story of Deborah, who was promoted to a position in nonprofit leadership, only to find her hopes dashed by the day-to-day realities of the work. Fast-forward to the future and imagine that Deborah has a blueprint for practice. She doesn't have to go through years of having good and bad overseers to walk into her position with some sense of what to do as a nonprofit leader. Enter leadership standpoints. It's a leadership theory that's both descriptive of leadership excellence in the nonprofit sector and prescriptive in organizing a flexible set of actions, characteristics, and general terminologies for future leaders to use.

7.1 An Aspirational Framework

Being a high-level framework that's intended to guide practice, leadership standpoints don't provide exact details about how much one might allocate for, say, an annual budget with portions going to fundraising, marketing, or human resources. It does, however, provide overarching guidance on both why and how to go about such tasks. As some directions one's thoughts might take in thinking through a budget, a leader could think about the many standpoints at play with finances, seeking and distributing insights into this process from the center while attending to the social and ecological impacts these numerical decisions will have from a number of positions. In this sense, leadership standpoints forward an aspirational model with attention to its own limitations built in. It can't provide exact answers to many specific questions, but it can be drawn on to see where one and others are and, more importantly, where everyone might go in examining and practicing as many standpoints as possible relative to a topic.

A driving motivation for this project was to construct an approach that can guide nonprofit professionals' practice, since frameworks are more accessible and memorable to participants than leadership development that provides disconnected information and disparate experiences. One of our participants described this desire for integration as inherent to those seeking leadership development in the first place. Speaking about another fellow, we were told: "I think that she was just needing to put all of the ingredients that she had together in a way that she could also see it and then go and talk to the rest of her team about it." Similarly, we also heard the training described as tying "everything into a bow" and "boil[ing] leadership skills down."

Consistent with undercurrents in the public sector, moving from deficit framings for development to an asset lens with communities is critical – in this context, thinking about what works from the perspective of emerging leaders already reflective of and enmeshed in nonprofit practice.[55] This Element has worked largely from this lens, focusing on what might be affirmed, sustained, and aspired to in leadership development (see Figure 7).

7.2 Following the Currents

Leadership standpoints and other leadership theories and practices around the world should be connected. This framework doesn't arrive in a vacuum. It builds on many extant contributions and can work alongside these other ideas. Since "many of the gravest problems in our world – from climate change to inequality to child abuse – are rooted in the misuse of power" (Arora, Elawar, & Cheng 2019: 39), paramount among these is an emphasis on anti-authoritarianism. In fact, "research from multiple fields suggests that throughout human history, leaders ascended the hierarchy through one of two strategies: dominance (using force or coercion to gain control) or prestige (demonstrating competence and generosity so others follow of their own volition)" (McClanahan 2020: 1). In this respect, leadership standpoints firmly promote the latter strategy.

Different than leaders using dominance and force in their practices, those applying leadership standpoints could also be considered "systems leaders." These leaders "apply an unusual combination of skills and attributes to mobilize large-scale action for systems change. Like many leaders, they tend to be smart, ambitious visionaries with strong skills in management and execution. Unlike traditional leaders, they are often humble, good listeners, and skilled facilitators who can successfully engage stakeholders with highly divergent priorities and

---

[55] "Professor John McKnight: About John McKnight and the asset-based community development institute," Minnesota Governor's Council on Developmental Disabilities, YouTube, August 26, 2014, www.youtube.com/watch?v=27fCAK1AUpE.

Figure 7 Elevating leadership. Photo courtesy of the NYCTLF.

perspectives" (Dreier, Nabarro, & Nelson 2019). For those who have never given much thought to these matters, leadership standpoints flow with these currents. The emphasis on multiplicity and social and ecological compassion within leadership standpoints also relates to *"multidimensional authenticity"* that recognizes "the many-layered and evolving nature of the self" living among others (Arora, Elawar, & Cheng 2019: 41). Since leaders often have the most influence in constructing and sustaining organizational culture, they need to be skilled at performing multiple roles (including manager and administrator), promoting an ecology of collaboration and participation (Golensky & Hager 2020: 81, 85, 125). The practices that can work with these themes are central to modern leadership.

7.3 Strategic Leadership Planning

Leadership standpoints aren't simply a nice add-on to nonprofit activities but should be at the core of strategic planning. In essence, "research shows that the single biggest cause of work burnout is not work overload, but working too long without experiencing your own personal development" (Kegan & Lahey 2016: 2). When leadership development can so easily be the first item cut from a budget, the case for systematic and structural support is lost. NYCTLF instructor Lori Roth Gale highlights in her workshop on organizational devel-opment that both motivation to learn and urgency to learn are critical variables. One of our interviewees made this interest abundantly clear: "there's just not enough leadership programming that's available and affordable – meaningful programming that's available and affordable to people working in the sector. And given the scope of problems that people are trying to solve, it's like your handicapping us from the outset ... we need to do better for people."

These problems surface in the public sector more broadly, too. In a study of government workers, one project found that "Nearly 9 out of 10 senior executives surveyed worldwide felt it was 'extremely important' for them to work collaboratively across boundaries," yet "fewer than 1 in 10 felt they had the skills to do so effectively."[56] Having a guiding leadership theory pointing to these gaps can help those in these fields make a more assertive case for leadership development in general.

Leadership workshops are not enough. They must be supplemented across time with support for helping emerging leaders move successfully into and through positions with realistic guidance. Indeed, leadership development generally falls into four categories: individual skill development; socialization into an organization's vision and values; strategic interventions targeting some type of major organizational change; or targeted approaches addressing organizational opportunities or challenges – with individual skill development usually receiving the lion's share of attention (Conger 2010: 286). The latter three approaches underscore how leadership development needs more strategic and across-the-board attention. Leading interactively from the center requires a responsiveness that's felt at both individual and collective levels.

Leadership standpoints elevate many positionalities, so programs can perform this expectation in practice by constructing a variety of leadership development experiences. Landles-Cobb, Kramer, and Milway (2015: para. 35) describe this continuing need in terms of mitigating turnover and developing emerging leaders: "the CEO and executive team need to define the organization's future leadership requirements, identify promising internal candidates, and provide the right doses of stretch assignments, mentoring, formal training, and performance assessment to grow their capabilities" (see also Burkhauser & Nayak 2013).

In particular, quality, holistic mentoring conceived through open communication, validations of worth, co-creative learning, positional attention and structural advocacy toward access and opportunity, as well as multiple (not simply single) reflexive relationships can act as transformative tools for advancing social justice in and outside of organizations (Murrell & Blake-Beard

---

[56] "How government workers can collaborate across boundaries," Center for Creative Leadership, www.ccl.org/articles/leading-effectively-articles/government-all-talk-and-no-action/? utm_campaign=1-LeadersAtAllLevels%2C2-LE_Article%2C3-GLP&utm_medium=social&u tm_source=linkedin&utm_content=1569855001.

2017). Leadership standpoints also fit with calls to take "a simple shift away from detailed and event-specific decision-making and toward values and valuing [that] produces a powerful change in board leadership," especially in driving the creation of active, guiding policies (Carver 2006: 40). These connections call for more strategic and less ad hoc attention to distributed leadership development grounded in value-driven frameworks. Nonprofit staff should thus build opportunities for developing the three main dimensions and eleven corresponding themes of leadership standpoints into their strategic planning.

7.4 The Digital Future

Writing this project partly took place during the most disruptive event to occur globally in a generation, the COVID-19 pandemic. During this time, it was common to hear that the world would not be the same place after as it was before. One way that this has certainly played out is in the grand shift online that almost everyone on this planet had to make during the outbreak. Where in a pre-COVID-19 world our move into digital spaces was already proceeding exponentially, a post-COVID-19 world has made this acceleration total. We are in the midst of a "fourth industrial revolution" – the fastest period of change humankind has ever confronted – where "no single genius or group of geniuses are capable of even getting their collective brains around everything that is coming at us" (Bonime-Blanc 2020: 6–7, 252), so "collaborative groups of virtual and actual cross-disciplinary experts" (33) and others will need to work together to solve the planet's most pressing issues.

Such events only accentuate the need for leadership standpoints to address the volatile, uncertain, complex, and ambiguous world in which we're living (Horney, Pasmore, & O'Shea 2010: 34). Indeed, leadership standpoints offer exactly the kind of dynamic and attentive leadership best suited to a rapidly shifting environment and the multiplicity of stakeholders now reached across digital spaces.

As surfaced during this project, some incorporation of digital mobility can play a part in leadership development. As a newer means of doing this work well, the addition of mobile support and learning might enhance professional development and the transfer of learning.[57] Narayandas and Moldoveanu (2019: 40–48) focus these expectations on "the gap between the skills that executive development programs build and the skills that organizations require – particularly the interpersonal skills essential to thriving in today's flat,

---

[57] See, for example, Safioo (www.safioo.com) for one means of doing so. For a widely used leadership development, peer-coaching platform also increasingly used, see Imperative (www .imperative.com).

networked, increasingly collaborative organizations," and how "most executives do not seem to take what they learn in the classroom and apply it to their jobs … The good news is that the growing assortment of online courses, social and interactive platforms, and learning tools from both traditional institutions and upstarts … offers a solution." Nonprofit leadership development must attend to the digital layers that human beings inhabit as forms of leadership standpoints worth stepping into. That said, while leaning into the digital is now a core competency, knowing its place and when to turn off will likely remain equally important.

7.5 Sequencing Implementation

For the challenges of leadership training programs focusing on racial and gender justice, it's also critical to think about the sequence for implementing leadership standpoints. Space training sessions over time (e.g. once every few weeks or once a month) rather than running rushed sessions (Abner et al. 2019; Lacerenza et al. 2017: 1686). Participants need time to soak in ideas about their own and others' standpoints and even more time to process how they will translate these insights to practice new standpoints. Having the thread of nonprofit leadership standpoints run through every learning session is essential.

Promising practices in leadership training more broadly should be connected to these efforts. From the programming side, leadership development involves six factors: "a thorough needs assessment, the selection of a suitable audience, the design of an appropriate infrastructure to support the initiative, the design and implementation of an entire learning system, an evaluation system, and the corresponding actions to reward success and improve on deficiencies" (Leskiw & Singh 2007: 444). These factors are beyond this project's scope but will remain critical for implementation. In terms of sequencing – and given these serious goals – Perry, Meehan, and Reinalt (2009: 10) also remind us to "*Have fun first.* Community building does not start in meetings, it starts with eating and talking and creating opportunities for people to build relationships." People are motivated by the ways they naturally engage in a variety of settings.

One of the biggest problems is what happens when a nonprofit fellowship or similar leadership development experience is over. If the learning doesn't drive sustained attention to leadership development after, the results may come up short. A fellow suggested that perhaps ending every session with an essential question (e.g. "what's different about you as a leader") could advance commitments extending the shelf-life of programming. One idea is to have those undergoing leadership development give back to such programs as a scheduled "teacher," through both online or offline programming – a best practice in a government leadership development program (Abner et al. 2019). Creating a website aligned with development efforts may also prove useful. Overall, part of a unique signature could be to make a post-certificate, lifelong commitment to remain networked with alumni and nonprofit leaders themselves as an ongoing knowledge source.

NYCTLF instructor Toby Thompkins (n.d.) reminds us that such learning must always be founded in but move beyond participants' worlds: "To move a leader away from a prescribed or self-constructed narrative they must be introduced to new leadership experiences that challenge their prevailing narrative and subsequent ways of being . . . Knowledge can change narratives but only experience can transform our narratives." Leadership standpoints are all about gaining the knowledge and experiences to step into new stories, while never letting go of the need for continuous learning, relearning, and an openness to surprises.

7.6 Challenges and Trust

Having heard from fellowship alumni that common language practices are often inadequate for the contemporary nonprofit landscape, one additional consideration that a theory for the next generation of nonprofit professionals brings into view is the terms that might best promote the field's future. Should we be dissatisfied with the term "nonprofit," for instance? That an entire field is defined in relation to the corporate sector by what it is *not*, versus what it is *for*, begs further questions worth investigating. I don't hope to address this question, but in considering leadership standpoints as a new framework I'd urge readers to consider if redefinitions of the sector should also be at play. One prompt may be to use "single-loop learning" (projects that contribute to one's field) and "double-loop learning" (projects that toggle back and forth with outside disciplines and practices that can inform and evolve one's field) (Argyris 1977) – in the spirit of applying the polymathic knowledge theme – to think about what terms from other locations (i.e. standpoints) could be adapted to present nonprofit contexts.

Before bringing this Element to a close, some qualifications. Every theory has its limits and, as important as leadership is, one limitation is that it can't contain everything that happens in nonprofit life. The potential to attribute leadership as the source for all problems or opportunities is a common fallacy in thinking about how organizations work. One of the fellows even noted: "I sometimes wonder if the problems are structural and I don't know if leadership can fix [them]." Leadership is only part of the picture, so stepping into a standpoint where humility about the effects of what one does is necessary. Another limitation of this project is that it sought to isolate a nonprofit leadership theory.

In our interviews, we heard that fellows thought that further comparisons with different forms of productive and unproductive leadership might help nonprofit leaders, including more distinctions between unconventional, conventional, or other forms or subforms of leadership (e.g. religious). These were beyond this project's purview but might prove useful in future work.

Given that the fellowship program at the center of this analysis comes from the New York Community Trust, I'd like to finally spotlight the concept of "trust." Given all that's been covered, I can think of no better word to describe the ultimate goal of leadership standpoints. Trust is a long-standing theme in the leadership literature and one of the most powerful intangible assets connected to tangible negative or positive consequences (Bonime-Blanc 2020: 11).[58] As Marcus Walton highlights, in particular, "If you look up [the term] 'philanthropy,' it is love of all humankind. Humanity is at the core of grantmaking, and any meaningful grantmaking process intends to uplift and improve the conditions of our collective humanity."[59] In this spirit, as a theory and practices for leadership development and leadership in action, leadership standpoints seek to build greater trust in oneself, exhibiting more bravery, vision, compassion, eclecticism, wellness, and more. At the same time, this is all in the service of building greater trust with others, creating diverse communities, facilitating distributed decision-making, and inspiring confidence in people's abilities. As an open-ended project, I now put my trust in you, dear readers, to discover, apply, and evolve leadership standpoints for future generations.

---

[58] "Measuring the return on character," *Harvard Business Review*, April 2015, https://hbr.org/2015/04/measuring-the-return-on-character.

[59] "A lesson in leadership: An interview with GEO CEO Marcus Walton," The Bridgespan Group, April 27, 2020: para. 10, www.bridgespan.org/insights/library/philanthropy/lesson-in-leadership-marcus-walton#fb.

References

Abner, G., Perry, J. L., Morrison, J. K., & Valdez, B. (2019). *Preparing the Next Generation of Federal Leaders: Agency-Based Leadership Development Programs*. IBM Center for the Business of Government report. www.businessofgovernment.org/sites/default/files/Preparing%20the%20Next%20Generation%20of%20Federal%20Leaders.pdf.

Aguinis, H. & Kraiger, K. (2009). Benefits of training and development for individuals and teams, organizations, and society. *Annual Review of Psychology*, 60, 451–474.

Alcoff, L. (1991). The problem of speaking for others. *Cultural Critique*, 20, 5–32.

Allard S. & Reuter, B. (n.d.). Cultivating the next generation of nonprofit leaders in metro areas. Race to Lead. http://racetolead.org/cultivating-the-next-generation-of-nonprofit-leaders-in-metro-areas/.

Alvesson, M. & Einola, K. (2019). Warning for excessive positivity: Authentic leadership and other traps in leadership studies. *The Leadership Quarterly*, 30, 383–395.

Appelbaum, S. H., Audet, L., & Miller, J. C. (2003). Gender and leadership? Leadership and gender? A journey through the landscape of theories. *Leadership and Organization Development Journal*, 24, 43–51.

Argyris, C. (1977). Double loop learning in organizations. *Harvard Business Review*. https://hbr.org/1977/09/double-loop-learning-in-organizations.

Arora, A., Elawar, M., & Cheng, S. (2019). Socially conscious leadership: An integrated model. *Journal of Leadership Studies*, 13, 38–43.

Ayman, R. & Korabik, K. (2010). Leadership: Why gender and culture matter. *American Psychologist*, 65, 157–170.

Bardy, R. (2018). *Rethinking Leadership: A Human Centered Approach to Management Ethics*. New York: Routledge.

Baxter, L. A. & Montgomery, B. M. (1996). *Relating: Dialogues and Dialectics*. New York: Guilford Press.

Beck, D. E. & Cowan, C. C. (2006). *Spiral Dynamics: Mastering Values, Leadership and Change*. Malden, MA: Blackwell.

Beebe, S. A., Mottet, T. P., & Roach, K. D. (2012). *Training and Development: Communicating for Success*, 2nd ed. Upper Saddle River, NJ: Pearson Higher Ed.

Bennis, W. & Thomas, R. (2002). Crucibles of leadership. *Harvard Business Review*. https://hbr.org/2002/09/crucibles-of-leadership.

Biech, E. (2017). *The Art and Science of Training*. Alexandria, VA: ATD Press.

Bogart, A. & Landau, T. (2005). *The Viewpoints Book*. New York: Theatre Communications Group.

Bonime-Blanc, A. (2020). *Gloom to Boom: How Leaders Transform Risk into Resilience and Value*. New York: Routledge.

Booth, W. C. (2004). *The Rhetoric of Rhetoric: The Quest for Effective Communication*. Malden, MA: Blackwell.

Bowell, T. (n.d.). Feminist standpoint theory. *Internet Encyclopedia of Philosophy*. www.iep.utm.edu/fem-stan/.

Brimhall, K. C. (2019). Inclusion and commitment as key pathways between leadership and nonprofit performance. *Nonprofit Management and Leadership*, *30*, 31–49.

Buller, J. L. (2013). *Positive Academic Leadership: How to Stop Putting Out Fires and Start Making a Difference*. Hoboken, NJ: Wiley.

Burkhauser, L. & Nayak, P. (2013). Nonprofit leadership development toolkit. The Bridgespan Group. www.bridgespan.org/insights/library/leadership-development/nonprofit-leadership-development-toolkit.

Cameron, K. S., Quinn, R. E., DeGraff, J., & Thakor, A. V. (2014). *Competing Values Leadership*. Northampton, MA: Edward Elgar.

Carver, J. (2006). *Boards That Make a Difference: A New Design for Leadership in Nonprofit and Public Organizations*. San Francisco, CA: Jossey-Bass.

Case, P., Turnbull, S., & Khakwani, S. (2012). Introduction: The emerging case for worldly leadership. In S. Turnbull, P. Case, G. Edwards, D. Schedlitzki, & P. Simpson, eds., *Worldly Leadership: Alternative Wisdoms for a Complex World*. London: Palgrave Macmillan, pp. 3–16.

Cecchi-Dimeglio, P. (2020). In times of anxiety, lead with "we" and "us." *MIT Sloane Management Review*, May 18. https://sloanreview.mit.edu/article/in-times-of-anxiety-lead-with-we-and-us/.

Chenok, D. J., Cooney, H., Kamensky, J. M., Keegan, M. J., & Piechowski, D. (2017). *Seven Drivers Transforming Government*. IBM Center for the Business of Government report. www.businessofgovernment.org/sites/default/files/Seven%20Drivers%20Transforming%20Government.pdf.

Collins, D. B. & Holton, E. F., III (2004). The effectiveness of managerial leadership development programs: A meta-analysis of studies from 1982 to 2001. *Human Resource Development Quarterly*, 15, 217–248.

Conger, J. A. (2010). Developing leadership talent: Delivering on the promise of structured programs. In R. Silzer & B. Dowell, eds., *Strategy Driven Talent Management: A Leadership Imperative*. San Francisco, CA: Jossey-Bass, pp. 281–312.

Credi, A. & Ainsworth, C. (2019). Transforming your culture with conversations. Center for Creative Leadership. https://cclwebinars.webvent.tv/webinar/3545.

Cubías, P. (n.d.). When our humanity guides our strategies. CompassPoint, www.compasspoint.org/blog/when-our-humanity-guides-our-strategies.

Daskal, L. (2016). 100 answers to the question: What is leadership? Inc. www.inc.com/lolly-daskal/100-answers-to-the-question-what-is-leadership.html.

De Pree, M. (2004). *Leadership Is an Art*. New York: Random House.

DeVelde, T., Vela, P., Schenker, J. et al. (2005). *A Scan of Health Leadership Development Programs for the Youth, Immigrant and Senior Communities of California*. Report for the California Endowment. www.leadershiplearning.org/system/files/Scan%20of%20Health%20LD%20Programs.pdf.

DiNapoli, T. P. (2019). *Nonprofit Organizations in New York State: Profile of Employment and Wages*. Office of the New York State Comptroller report.

Diner, S. J. (2017). *Universities and Their Cities: Urban Higher Education in America*. Baltimore, MD: Johns Hopkins University Press.

Dorfman, P. W., Hanges, P. J., & Brodbeck, F. C. (2004). Leadership and cultural variation: The identification of culturally endorsed leadership profiles. In R. J. House, P. J. Hanges, M. Javidan, P. W. Dorfman, & V. Gupta, eds., *Culture, Leadership, and Organizations: The GLOBE Study of 62 Societies*. Thousand Oaks, CA: Sage, 669–719.

Dow, B. J. & Tonn, M. B. (1993). "Feminine style" and political judgment in the rhetoric of Ann Richards. *Quarterly Journal of Speech*, 79, 286–302.

Dreier, L., Nabarro, D., & Nelson, J. (2019). Systems leadership can change the world – but what exactly is it? World Economic Forum. www.weforum.org/agenda/2019/09/systems-leadership-can-change-the-world-but-what-does-it-mean/.

Duhigg, C. (2016). What Google learned from its quest to build the perfect team. *New York Times Magazine*, February 28. https://mobile.nytimes.com/2016/02/28/magazine/what-google-learned-from-its-quest-to-build-the-perfect-team.html?hp&action=click&pgtype=Homepage&clickSource=story-heading&module=photo-spot-region&region=top-news&WT.nav=top-news&_r=0&referer=.

Duke, S. (2017). The key to closing the gender gap? Putting more women in charge. World Economic Forum, November 2. www.weforum.org/agenda/2017/11/women-leaders-key-to-workplace-equality/.

Eagly, A. H. & Carli, L. L. (2003). The female leadership advantage: An evaluation of the evidence. *The Leadership Quarterly*, 14, 807–834.

Edmondson, A. C. (2019). *The Fearless Organization: Creating Psychological Safety in the Workplace for Learning, Innovation, and Growth*. Hoboken, NJ: Wiley.

Epstein, D. (2019). *Range: Why Generalists Triumph in a Specialized World.* New York: Penguin.

Eva, N., Cox, J. W., Herman, H. M., & Lowe, K. B. (2019). From competency to conversation: A multi-perspective approach to collective leadership development. *The Leadership Quarterly*, 1–14. www.sciencedirect.com/science/article/pii/S1048984318308853?via%3Dihub.

Fogg, B. J. (2008). Mass interpersonal persuasion: An early view of a new phenomenon. *International Conference on Persuasive Technology*, 5033, 23–34.

Foss, S. (2018). *Rhetorical Criticism: Exploration and Practice.* Long Grove, IL: Waveland.

Freire, P. (1970). *Pedagogy of the Oppressed.* New York: Seabury Press.

Fulton, B. R., Oyakawa, M., & Wood, R. L. (2019). Critical standpoint: Leaders of color advancing racial equality in predominantly white organizations. *Nonprofit Management and Leadership*, 30, 255–276.

Gale, L. R. (2018). Diagnosing the organization. New York Community Trust Fellows program, November 9.

Getha-Taylor, H., Fowles, J., Silvia, C., & Merritt, C. C. (2015). Considering the effects of time on leadership development: A local government training evaluation. *Public Personnel Management*, 44, 295–316.

Gladwell, M. (2005). *Blink: The Power of Thinking Without Thinking.* New York: Little, Brown and Company.

Goleman, D. (2006). *Emotional Intelligence.* New York: Bantam.

Golensky, M. & Hager, M. (2020). *Strategic Leadership and Management in Nonprofit Organizations: Theory and Practice.* New York: Oxford University Press.

Grant, H. M., Scearce, D., & Flower, N. (2010). Social networks for social change. Monitor Institute. www.slideshare.net/workingwikily/social-networks-for-social-change-wsp-166.

Gray, A. (2019). The bias of "professionalism" standards. *Stanford Social Innovation Review.* https://ssir.org/articles/entry/the_bias_of_professionalism_standards#.

Grint, K. (2010). *Leadership: A Very Short Introduction.* New York: Oxford University Press.

Gronn, P. (2002). Distributed leadership as a unit of analysis. *The Leadership Quarterly*, 13, 423–451.

Guest, G., Bunce, A., & Johnson, L. (2006). How many interviews are enough? An experiment with data saturation and variability. *Field Methods*, 18, 59–82.

Harding, S., ed. (2004). *The Feminist Standpoint Theory Reader: Intellectual and Political Controversies.* New York: Routledge.

Hargreaves, A. & Fink, F. (2012). *Sustainable Leadership*. San Francisco: Jossey-Bass.

Heifetz, R. A., Grashow, A., & Linsky, M. (2009). *The Practice of Adaptive Leadership*. Cambridge, MA: Harvard Business Press.

Hernez-Broome, G. & Hughes, R. J. (2004). Leadership development: Past, present, and future. *Human Resource Planning*, 27, 24–32.

Holt, J. (2019). Remember the "10,000 hours" rule for success? Forget about it. *New York Times*, May 28. www.nytimes.com/2019/05/28/books/review/david-epstein-range.html.

Holzman, L. (2017). *Vygotsky at Work and Play*. New York: Routledge.

Horney, N., Pasmore, B., & O'Shea, T. (2010). Leadership agility: A business imperative for a VUCA world. *People and Strategy*, 33, 32–38.

Hunter, T. (n.d.). Understanding viewpoints. Dramatics. https://dramatics.org/understanding-viewpoints/.

Jackson, S. & Aakhus, M. (2014). Becoming more reflective about the role of design in communication. *Journal of Applied Communication Research*, 42, 125–134.

Jacobs, G., Van Witteloostuijn, A., & Christe-Zeyse, J. (2013). A theoretical framework of organizational change. *Journal of Organizational Change Management*, 26, 772–792.

Jay, J. & Grant, G. (2017). *Breaking Through Gridlock: The Power of Conversation in a Polarized World*. Oakland, CA: Berrett-Koehler Publishers.

Kanter, R. M. (2011). Managing yourself: Zoom in, zoom out. *Harvard Business Review*. https://hbr.org/2011/03/managing-yourself-zoom-in-zoom-out.

Katz, D. & Kahn, R. L. (1978). *The Social Psychology of Organizations*. New York: Wiley.

Kay, R. (1994). The artistry of leadership: An exploration of the leadership process in voluntary not-for-profit organizations. *Nonprofit Management and Leadership*, 4, 285–300.

Kegan, R. & Lahey, L. L. (2016). *An Everyone Culture: Becoming a Deliberately Developmental Organization*. Cambridge, MA: Harvard Business Review Press.

Kuhn, K. (2016). Ken Blanchard: Business contributions and leadership model. Study.com. https://study.com/academy/lesson/ken-blanchard-business-contributions-leadership-model.html.

Lacerenza, C. N., Reyes, D. L., Marlow, S. L., Joseph, D. L., & Salas, E. (2017). Leadership training design, delivery, and implementation: A meta-analysis. *Journal of Applied Psychology*, 102, 1686–1718.

Landles-Cobb, L., Kramer K., & Milway, K. S. (2015). The nonprofit leadership development deficit. *Stanford Social Innovation Review.* https://ssir.org/art icles/entry/the_nonprofit_leadership_development_deficit.

Le, V. (2019). It's time funders take nonprofit leadership turnover seriously. Nonprofit AF, November 10. https://nonprofitaf.com/2019/11/its-time-funders-take-nonprofit-leadership-turnover-seriously/.

Lencioni, P. (2006). *The Five Dysfunctions of a Team.* Hoboken, NJ: Wiley.

Leskiw, S. L. & Singh, P. (2007). Leadership development: Learning from best practices. *Leadership and Organization Development Journal*, 28, 444–464.

Lilienfeld, S. O., Sauvigné, K. C., Lynn, S. J., Cautin, R. L., Latzman, R. D., & Waldman, I. D. (2015). Fifty psychological and psychiatric terms to avoid: A list of inaccurate, misleading, misused, ambiguous, and logically confused words and phrases. *Frontiers in Psychology*, 6, 1–15.

Lindstrom, N. (2018). Nonprofits unprepared for exodus of baby boomers, Robert Morris University report warns. *AP News*, January 29. https://apnews .com/article/30136a08632d42bb8deb992fcb84a537.

Lobell, J., Sikka, M., & Sauvage-Mar, C. (2009). What makes a difference in leadership development? A view from the field. *Nonprofit Quarterly*, December 21. https://nonprofitquarterly.org/what-makes-a-difference-in-leadership-development-a-view-from-the-field/.

Low, J. (2019). A pragmatic definition of the concept of theoretical saturation. *Sociological Focus*, 52, 131–139.

Lunenburg, F. C. (2010). Leader-member exchange theory: Another perspective on the leadership process. *International Journal of Management, Business, and Administration*, 13, 1–5.

Marturano, J. (2014). *Finding the Space to Lead: A Practical Guide to Mindful Leadership*. New York: Bloomsbury.

Maslach, C. & Leiter, M. P. (2008). Reversing burnout. *Stanford Social Innovation Review*. https://ssir.org/articles/entry/reversing_burnout.

Maurrasse, D. J. (2001). *Beyond the Campus: How Colleges and Universities Form Partnerships with Their Communities*. New York: Routledge.

McCauley, C. D., Van Velsor, E., & Ruderman, M. (2010). Introduction: Our view of leadership development. In E. Van Velsor, C. D. McCauley, & M. N. Ruderman, eds., *The Handbook of Leadership Development*. San Francisco, CA: Jossey-Bass, pp. 1–22.

McClanahan, K. J. (2020). Viva la evolution: Using dual-strategies theory to explain leadership in modern organizations. *The Leadership Quarterly*, 31, 1–13.

Mook, M. N. (2019). The nonprofit gender gap. *Forbes*, February 14. www
.forbes.com/sites/forbesnonprofitcouncil/2019/02/14/the-nonprofit-gender-
gap-how-to-get-the-female-leadership-you-need/?sh=61ee3b026a96.

Murrell, A. J. & Blake-Beard, S., eds. (2017). *Mentoring Diverse Leaders:
Creating Change for People, Processes, and Paradigms*. New York:
Routledge.

Narayandas, D. & Moldoveanu, M. (2019). The future of leadership development. *Harvard Business Review*. https://hbr.org/2019/03/the-future-of-
leadership-development.

Never, B. (2016). The changing context of nonprofit management in the United
States. In D. O. Renz, ed., *The Jossey-Bass Handbook of Nonprofit
Leadership and Management*. Hoboken, NJ: Wiley, pp. 80–101.

Nipper, D. (2019). Vision for the future of Rockwood. Rockwood Leadership
Institute. https://rockwoodleadership.org/vision-future-rockwood/.

Norley, P. & D'Amato, C. (2019). Major gaps in training and coaching hobble
nonprofit success. *The Chronicle of Philanthropy*, September 6. www
.philanthropy.com/article/Major-Gaps-in-Training-and/247082.

Northouse, P. (2018). *Leadership: Theory and Practice*. Thousand Oaks, CA:
Sage.

Oppenheim, P. (2017). Changing leadership dynamics in nonprofit organizations. Phillips Oppenheim website. www.phillipsoppenheim.com/tidbits/
changing-leadership-dynamics-in-nonprofit-organizations/9/.

Ospina S. & Sorenson, G. L. (2006). A constructionist lens on leadership:
Charting new territory. In G. R. Goethals & G. L. Sorenson, eds., *The
Quest for a General Theory of Leadership*. Northampton, MA: Edward
Elgar, pp. 188–204.

Palfrey, J. (2018). *Safe Spaces, Brave Spaces: Diversity and Free Expression in
Education*. Cambridge, MA: MIT Press.

Pearce, C. L. & Conger, J. A. (2002). *Shared Leadership: Reframing the Hows
and Whys of Leadership*. Thousand Oaks, CA: Sage.

Pearce, W. B. (2009). *Making Social Worlds: A Communication Perspective*.
Malden, MA: Blackwell.

Pernick, R. (2001). Creating a leadership development program: Nine essential
tasks. *Public Personnel Management*, 30, 429–444.

Perry, E., Meehan, D., & Reinelt, C. (2009). *Developing a Racial Justice and
Leadership Framework to Promote Racial Equity, Address Structural
Racism, and Heal Racial and Ethnic Divisions in Communities*. Report for
The W.K. Kellogg Foundation. The Center for Ethical Leadership. www
.leadershiplearning.org/system/files/Racial%20Equity%20and%
20Leadership%20Scan.pdf.

Pettegrew, L. (2016). A delicate balance: When the researcher is also an interventionist in healthcare settings. In J. Waldeck & D. Seibold, eds., *Consulting That Matters*. New York: Peter Lang, pp. 305–318.

Reinelt, C. & Fried, M. (2018a). *New York Community Trust Fellows Program Evaluation: An Impact Assessment Report*.

Reinelt, C. & Fried, M. (2018b). *NYCT Leadership Fellows Program Summary of Program Recommendations*.

Renz, D. O. & Herman, R. D. (2016). Understanding nonprofit effectiveness. In D. O. Renz, ed., *The Jossey-Bass Handbook of Nonprofit Leadership and Management*. Hoboken, NJ: Wiley, pp. 274–292.

Rolková, M. & Farkašová, V. (2015). The features of participative management style. *Procedia Economics and Finance*, 23, 1383–1387.

Rosener, J. B. (1990). Ways women lead. *Harvard Business Review*. https://hbr .org/1990/11/ways-women-lead.

Roy, K., Zvonkovic, A., Goldberg, A., Sharp, E., & LaRossa, R. (2015). Sampling richness and qualitative integrity: Challenges for research with families. *Journal of Marriage and Family*, 77, 243–260.

Saldaña, J. (2015). *The Coding Manual for Qualitative Researchers*. Thousand Oaks, CA: Sage.

Sánchez, L. (2010). Positionality. In B. Warf, ed., *Encyclopedia of Geography*. Thousand Oaks, CA: Sage, p. 2258.

Sasnett, B. & Ross, T. (2007). Leadership frames and perceptions of effectiveness among health information management program directors. *Perspectives in Health Information Management*, 4, 1–15.

Saunders, B., Sim, J., Kingstone, T. et al. (2018). Saturation in qualitative research: Exploring its conceptualization and operationalization. *Quality and Quantity*, 52, 1893–1907.

Schenker J. & Perry, E. (2005). *Multiple Styles of Leadership: Increasing the Participation of People of Color in the Leadership of the Nonprofit Sector*. Report for The Annie E. Casey Foundation. www.leadershiplearning.org /system/files/Final_AECF_Web_0.pdf.

Schwartz, T. & McCarthy, C. (2017). Manage your energy, not your time. *Harvard Business Review*. https://hbr.org/2007/10/manage-your-energy-not-your-time.

Seidle, B., Fernandez, S., & Perry, J. L. (2016). Do leadership training and development make a difference in the public sector? A panel study. *Public Administration Review*, 76, 603–613.

Sperrazza, C. (2019). New York Community Trust Leadership Fellows: Next generation of non-profiteers get ready to take the helm. New York Community Trust Newsroom, October 24. www.nycommunitytrust.org

/newsroom/new-york-community-trust-leadership-fellows-next-generation-of-non-profiteers-get-ready-to-take-the-helm/.

Stromberg, J. & Caswell, E. (2015). Why the Myers-Briggs test is totally meaningless. *Vox*, October 8. www.vox.com/2014/7/15/5881947/myers-briggs-personality-test-meaningless.

Thompkins, T. (n.d.). Transforming our narratives: Good governance in African cities. Unpublished manuscript.

Tierney, T. J. (2006). The nonprofit sector's leadership deficit. The Bridgespan Group. www.bridgespan.org/insights/library/leadership-development/non profit-sectors-leadership-deficit.

van der Wusten, H. ed. (1998). *The Urban University and Its Identity: Roots, Location, Roles*. Berlin: Springer.

Vogel, B., Reichard, R. J., Batistič, S., & Černe, M. (2020). A bibliometric review of the leadership development field: How we got here, where we are, and where we are headed. *The Leadership Quarterly*, 101381, 1–20. www.sciencedirect.com/science/article/pii/S1048984320300084.

Waisanen, D. J. (2019). Communication training's higher calling: Using a civic frame to promote transparency and elevate the value of services. In J. D. Wallace & D. Becker, eds., *Handbook of Communication Training*. New York: Routledge, pp. 21–35.

Waisanen, D. J. (2021). *Improv for Democracy: How to Bridge Differences and Develop the Communication and Leadership Skills Our World Needs*. Albany, NY: State University of New York Press.

Waldeck J. & Seibold, D. (2016). Preface. In J. Waldeck & D. Seibold, eds., *Consulting That Matters*. New York: Peter Lang, pp. ix–xiii.

Watts, D. (2011). *Everything Is Obvious*: *Once You Know the Answer*. New York: Crown.

Watzlawick, P., Beavin, J., & Jackson, D. (1967). *Pragmatics of Human Communication*. New York: Norton.

Way, C. (2012). What is sustainability leadership? ATD. www.td.org/insights/what-is-sustainability-leadership.

Weick K. E. & Sutcliffe, K. M. (2015). *Managing the Unexpected: Sustained Performance in a Complex World*. Hoboken, NJ: Wiley.

The White House Project. (2009). *The White House Project: Benchmarking Women's Leadership*. New York: The White House Project. www.in.gov/icw/files/benchmark_wom_leadership.pdf.

Acknowledgements

If it weren't for the New York Community Trust Leadership Fellowship, this project would not have been possible. All my thanks to staff Michael Seltzer (the founding director of the fellowship), Gaurav Bawa (the former deputy director), and Shelly Ho (the communications officer for the program) at the Marxe School of Public and International Affairs, Patricia A. Swann (senior program officer at the New York Community Trust), and Shana Kieran-Kaufman for her outstanding work as my research assistant on this project. I'd also like to thank Toby Thompkins, Lori Roth Gale, Fred Lane, John Casey, Nancy Aries, Rachél Fester, Karen Noble, and Marti Fischer for their generous and detailed feedback on this Element's early drafts. This project was supported by a grant from the New York Community Trust Leadership Fellowship.

Cambridge Elements ☰

Public and Nonprofit Administration

Andrew Whitford
University of Georgia
Andrew Whitford is Alexander M. Crenshaw Professor of Public Policy in the School of Public and International Affairs at the University of Georgia. His research centers on strategy and innovation in public policy and organization studies.

Robert Christensen
Brigham Young University
Robert Christensen is professor and George Romney Research Fellow in the Marriott School at Brigham Young University. His research focuses on prosocial and antisocial behaviors and attitudes in public and nonprofit organizations.

About the Series
The foundation of this series are cutting-edge contributions on emerging topics and definitive reviews of keystone topics in public and nonprofit administration, especially those that lack longer treatment in textbook or other formats. Among keystone topics of interest for scholars and practitioners of public and nonprofit administration, it covers public management, public budgeting and finance, nonprofit studies, and the interstitial space between the public and nonprofit sectors, along with theoretical and methodological contributions, including quantitative, qualitative and mixed-methods pieces.

The Public Management Research Association
The Public Management Research Association improves public governance by advancing research on public organizations, strengthening links among interdisciplinary scholars, and furthering professional and academic opportunities in public management.

Cambridge Elements $\equiv$

Public and Nonprofit Administration

Elements in the Series

Printed in the United States
by Baker & Taylor Publisher Services